MW00937212

Dirty Little Secret

Dirty Little Secret

◆

What No One Ever Tells You About Internet Adult Entertainment Industry

Nadeem Brown

iUniverse, Inc.
New York Lincoln Shanghai

Dirty Little Secret
What No One Ever Tells You About Internet Adult Entertainment Industry

Copyright © 2005 by Nadeem Brown

All rights reserved. No part of this book may be used or reproduced by any means, graphic, electronic, or mechanical, including photocopying, recording, taping or by any information storage retrieval system without the written permission of the publisher except in the case of brief quotations embodied in critical articles and reviews.

iUniverse books may be ordered through booksellers or by contacting:

iUniverse
2021 Pine Lake Road, Suite 100
Lincoln, NE 68512
www.iuniverse.com
1-800-Authors (1-800-288-4677)

ISBN-13: 978-0-595-37421-2 (pbk)
ISBN-13: 978-0-595-81814-3 (ebk)
ISBN-10: 0-595-37421-2 (pbk)
ISBN-10: 0-595-81814-5 (ebk)

Printed in the United States of America

Whilst we hope you find the contents of this book interesting and informative, the contents are for general information purposes only and do not constitute advice. We believe the contents to be true and accurate as at the date of writing but can give no assurances or warranty regarding the accuracy, currency or applicability of any of the contents in relation to specific situations and particular circumstances. As such, the contents should not be relied upon and readers should not act upon this information without seeking appropriate professional advice. Readers should always seek the advice of an appropriately qualified person in the reader's home jurisdiction. Publisher and Author of this book assume no responsibility for information contained in this book and disclaims all liability in respect of such information. In addition, none of the content of this book will form any part of any contract between us or constitutes an offer by us. Specific disclaimers may apply in addition to certain content or parts of the book.

Any links to third party websites are provided solely for the purpose of your convenience. Links made to other sites are made at your own risk and author and publisher of this book accept no liability for any web sites. Further, a web site link, company, or firm mention in this book does not mean that author endorses or accepts any responsibility for the content or the use of such website. Further, author does not give any guarantee regarding the quality, safety, suitability or reliability of any of them or any of the material contained in them.

Contents

How to make money
on the Internet

The title of this chapter is an answer to the most frequently asked question I heard at InterNext Expo (The adult entertainment expo), both in the hallways and in the sessions. Yes, the Internet is cool, but how do you make money? This is the question that the Have-Nots ask those that Have, or another way, that the Get-Nots ask those who claim to Get. I am so smug in the belief that I can answer the question that I'll ramble my way there, knowing that it's so pregnant that you'll read all the way to the end to hear what I learned and experienced at expo just to get an answer to this question that has so many people wondering.

THE $12 BILLION INTERNET PORNOGRAPHY INDUSTRY

The number of pornographic Web pages has grown 3,000 percent since 1998. There were 14 million pornographic Web pages in 1998 and 420 million today. "The adult Internet works at laser speed, and that's what makes it exciting," said Tom Hymes, a spokesman for the Free Speech Coalition, a lobbying group backed by the pornography industry.

HOW MUCH DO ADULT SITES REALLY MAKE?

This varies widely. A commercial website can cost anywhere from $150/month to well over $5,000 a month to operate. The website owner is charged for the commercial account, and also for transfer fees. How much material is accessed from a site. It's true that there is money to be made, however I don't think the public

1

perception of how much is very accurate. The advertisements for "operate an adult Website and make millions" are for the most part false. There are large sites out there making A LOT of money. But they are the exception, not the rule. There are certain parts of the business that work well—people who actually do live video in their own homes do well. Large pay sites do well. There are sites making millions, but. 95% of those make under $8,000 a month. It's really only the very top echelons that are making A LOT of money.

WHAT THIS BOOK WILL DO FOR YOU

I want to make it perfectly clear that this book will not be all things to all people. You will not, for example, find magic, get-rich-quick formulas in these pages. Being a successful Webmaster or businessperson, by any measure, is not easy.

Even if you are already a savvy surfer, comfortable in navigating your way around chat rooms, Thumbnail Gallery Posts, or the most complicated pay sites, you may need to acquire some basic business skills before launching your own Web site. Do your homework—sit down and really read this book.

In this book you will learn how to:

- Pick the best niche for yourself

- Start your own web site for reasonable cost

- Build your fortune in a business you comfortable with

- Run a business by not leaving your home

- Run a home business while keeping your day job

- Profit from unusual business ideas

- Advertise and Promote your web site using search engines

- Get a merchant credit card account so you can accept credit card charges by your customer

Any home business has many advantages over a business in which you rent space to conduct your profit-making activities. Most home business have no, or very little overhead. This means that more of every sales dollar stays in your pocket because you're not paying money for rent, storage space, or other occupancy needs.

More importantly to some people, a home business gives you independence. You can almost always choose your work hours, be they early or late. You don't have to conform to someone else's rigid schedule. You make your own schedule.

When thinking of a home business, remember that you may find it profitable to run two or more activities from your home. Why? Because this can ensure that you have income in both up and down economies. Your goal in opening your own home business is to have an independent income.

Why Should You Start An Adult Web Site?

Because Sex sells, especially to Web surfers

Internet porn a booming, billion-dollar industry

It's difficult to derive reliable figures from an industry that, despite flirtations with the mainstream, is made up of many small shops that prefer to keep a low profile. But the figures that exist paint a picture of a booming online field, fueled by the relatively low costs of setting up shop, fickle consumers in constant search of new thrills and the promise of quick profits.

"It's an enormous business…There's a lot of money to be made," said Sean Kaldor, an analyst with Nielsen/NetRatings which estimated that 34 million visited porn sites in August—about one in four Internet users in the United States.

The average user is "looking at 121 pages, going back six times and spending an hour and seven minutes every month looking at adult-related material," Kaldor said.

All that browsing has caused the number of pornography Web pages to soar during the past six years, with over 1.3 million sites serving up about 260 million pages of erotic content, according to a study released in September by the Seattle, Washington-based Web-filtering company N2H2.

N2H2's database of porn sites, a company spokesman said, includes many low-budget, fly-by-night and sometimes unscrupulous operators hoping to rake in their share of a market that the National Research Council estimates to be in the $1 billion range annually.

The council, which advises Congress on technology, issued a report in 2002 that predicts the online porn industry will grow to a $5-$7 billion business within five years.

Porn has been one of the few profitable Internet businesses from the start, employing thousands of people and generating millions in revenues for site owners, Web hosting companies and computer-hardware firms.

"It's all about dollar signs," says adult web site operator Jack Somers, 25.

Somers says he's making about $4,000 a month working on his porn sites about three hours a day. The rest of the time he's a freelance Web designer for non-adult businesses.

Like many adult web site operators, Somers makes money by signing up with a sponsor who owns pay sites. The sponsor gives Somers a few pictures to post for free on the Web, hoping some folks who see the free stuff will click through to the sponsor's site and buy memberships.

Somers gets a cut of every membership he helps generate.

"As long as I keep making money, I can't complain," he says, adding that most of his money comes from promoting a gay site even though he's straight and has a girlfriend.

"You have to stay with one niche that works well," he says. "The girlfriend doesn't care."

Experts say the industry has been on the forefront of many innovations that have been adopted by mainstream sites, such as new payment systems, ad revenue models, chat and broadband.

"One of the most interesting things is to watch how these sites pioneer new technologies," said Kaldor, the Nielsen/NetRatings analyst.

ONLINE ADULT ENTERTAINMENT INDUSTRY GROWS UP

Industry is showing signs of maturity.

Password services have sprung up, often charging an annual fee to deliver access to hundreds of small sites, which share the subscription revenues.

Large firms also have consolidated power by providing free content to smaller "affiliate" sites. The affiliates post the free content and then try to channel visitors to the large sites, which give the smaller sites a percentage of the fees paid by those who sign up.

Another way some adult Webmasters make money is by forwarding traffic to another porn site in return for a small per-consumer fee

A fourth trend is for adult sites to cater to niche audiences.

"There's a Web site for just about every kink," said Scott Fayner, who writes for LukeFord.com, a site that posts porn industry news and gossip.

Experts say tech advances and the growing use of broadband will fuel even more growth in the industry.

ADULT INDUSTRY AND THE FUTURE

Broadband. The implementation of fiber-optic cable, satellite and wireless antennae connections to the Internet are in limited existence now. These types of Internet delivery far surpass the capabilities of the telephone modem connection. The telephone or Dial-Up connection allows only a minimal amount of bits to pass through its skinny wires. A broadband connection passes bits too, but it is less like a skinny wire and more like a big pipe. The more that broadband is accepted and implemented, the more demanding the users of Internet porn will be. The surfer of the very near future will have a machine and a connection that allow them to download audio and video in real-time speed just like their television.

The collections of still images and video clips that many Adult sites consist of today will probably not attract the porn surfer of the future. More adventurous endeavors such as plot-based shows and artificially intelligent cyber dolls that interact with the surfer are going to have a real-time audience eventually. While the websites one sees on their cell phones now seem crude, mobile internet devices will only improve and deliver the same content as their bigger desktop and laptop versions. Internet technology is evolving faster than the telephone, radio and television ever did.

Porn will be there right on the future's cutting edge.

Like it or hate it, Internet porn is here to stay, Amsden said. And the key, said sex therapist Laura Berman, is to keep it in check.

"There's always a role for pornography and for fantasies, if it's used to the benefit of the couple," Berman said.

So how do I make money?

This chapter reveals several of the best, time-tested, revenue-generating ways to help get your moneymaking site started, and keep that money rolling in over the long-term.

ADULT VERIFICATION SYSTEM

An Adult Verification System (AVS) sets up a password protected entry for web sites that do not want their web sites to be "publicly accessible" to people under the age of 18. AVS systems benefit the webmasters by providing them a free age verification service for their sites. AVS systems benefit the surfer by issuing them an adult ID that allows them to access all the participating sites with one password. By signing up with an age verification system, you only have to verify your age once. After your age has been verified (if you are over 18) you will have access to hundreds of adult web sites worldwide! This is much better than having to verify your age with each different web site you enter, and paying a separate charge for each one. Most of the money is distributed to the participating adult sites to help them maintain their site, which can be very expensive. Part of the money goes to the company running the AVS

In addition to "doing the right thing" by keeping minors out of inappropriate areas of your site, signing up with a top-notch AVS is a great way to make money with your site. Webmasters who protect their sites with an AVS are paid a commission by that AVS for every surfer who signs up for a membership to the system. In most cases, AVS commissions will not result in enough revenue for you to retire for life, however, if you are willing to put in a little work promoting your site in the right market you could definitely end up with a significant supplement to your revenue.

AFFILIATE PROGRAMME

There are a number of reasons why affiliate programs can be an excellent way to start an Adult Web Site. Before we dive into the specifics let me explain how an affiliate program (and affiliate marketing in general) works.

An affiliate program is just another way for a company to sell its products. By signing up affiliates who will market the company's products for a commission, the company can effectively expand its sales force and market reach without adding employees or overhead. The more affiliates a company has, the more people selling its products and the more revenue the company makes. An affiliate is an individual (or a company) that signs up with an affiliate program with the intent of marketing the affiliate company's products on a commission basis. An affiliate is not an employee or a contractor. The affiliate receives no perks from the company other than the right to market or resell the company's products.

Thousands of companies have launched successful affiliate programs, from Internet giants like eBay and Amazon.com to traditional businesses like Hallmark and AT&T. The very fact that these kinds of companies have launched affiliate programs tells you that a well-managed affiliate program can do much for a company's bottom line.

If you're unfamiliar with how affiliate marketing works, here is the process:

1. First, you sign up with a company to market its products. Signing up usually involves registering at the company's Web site. The company will typically assign you a unique affiliate ID or tracking URL that you will use when marketing the product online.

2. Next, you market the product from your Web site or through other means of online advertising.

3. When someone clicks the link embedded with your affiliate ID, he or she is taken to the company's Web site to make the purchase. Using cookies or other digital tracking methods, the company notes your affiliate ID as the referring affiliate and pays you the commission if the customer buys.

There are several advantages to starting an affiliate marketing business:

- **Startup costs are minimal.** All affiliate programs let you sign on for free, which means your only costs to begin your business will be the money you spend on advertising the product. Some affiliate programs do charge a fee, but those affiliate programs are typically the ones that provide you with additional tools and assistance to help start your business. An example would be if the company provides you with a customized Web site from which to sell, you will probably be charged a fee, though the fee should be a fraction of what you would spend to build the site and develop products on your own.

- **You do not need your own product.** Since you are marketing someone else's products, you don't have to create or manufacturer a product of your own, which is often a huge barrier to entry for new entrepreneurs.

- **You have no distribution or customer service costs.** When an order is placed, the company handles delivery and customer service issues for you. This is especially nice if you are selling big-ticket items that require special shipping and handling or specialized products that lend themselves to customer hand-holding.

- **You can quickly begin making money.** One of the most appealing aspects of affiliate programs is how quickly you can begin making money. You can literally sign up as an affiliate and begin making money in minutes.

The bottom line is this: You can make a lot of money with affiliate programs if you pick a good product with mass appeal and do your part to promote it. As with any new business venture, it's all about marketing.

CLICK-THRU PROGRAMS

Many sites of all kinds use click-thrus. I've seen them on pay sites, AVS sites, and free sites alike. This is where the website is paid a tiny amount (typically anywhere from $ .02— .14) per click. You clicking on the link from their site, and linking to the pay site. Some of these are in the form of sponsor banners. I'm sure you've seen the pleas to "visit my sponsor. They keep us free" etc. Some are also in the form of text links. Usually a clickthru has rules for how a text link can appear. They do not want a surfer to get to their site by accident. They want the surfer to know where they are headed. Better chance then for a paid membership.

Some sites use text links in unethical ways. They make text links that look like they are part of their site. You go in and see "click here for free pictures", click there and find yourself out of the site. Usually, these sites also use "blind links". The URL you typically see in the lower left-hand border of your browser is replaced by whatever text they choose. I believe surfers should get a free choice of where to go. Not be directed there by a greedy Webmaster

Per Sigh-Up Programs

Under a per sign-up program webmasters are paid a set rate for every surfer who joins the sponsor's site after having been referred to the sponsor by the Webmaster. Most quality per sign-up programs pay between $25 and $50 per membership. Since most per sign-up programs tend to have fairly liberal promotional rules as to how and where webmasters may promote the sponsor's sites they are best used on AVS Web sites, TGPs and in exit consoles on free-access sites.

Partnership Programs

Each time a surfer purchases a membership to a sponsor's site after having been referred to the sponsor by a particular Webmaster, that webmasters is paid a percentage of the membership fee. Additionally, each time a surfer renews his membership with the sponsor, the Webmaster receives an additional commission. Most partnership commission rates are in the 40%-60% neighborhood. For example, if a surfer on your site clicks one of your sponsor's banner ads, visits the sponsor's site, and purchases a membership, you will receive anywhere from 40-60 percent of the membership fee. Each time this same surfer renews his membership with the sponsor you will receive an additional 40-60 percent of the membership fee, even if the surfer never visits your site again.

Many of the best affiliate programs in the online adult industry are listed in the *Down & Dirty Resource Guide* at the back of this book.

ONLINE ADULT STORES & RESELLER PROGRAMS

Many retail companies offer reseller programs for webmasters who operate sites related to the retailer's line of business. Visitors to a Web site that participate in a reseller program are able to purchase a variety of products such as adult toys, books, videos and DVDs from the participating webmaster's site. Once a purchase has been completed, all pertinent information is automatically sent to the retailer and the retailer fulfills the order. Webmasters who participate in reseller programs are generally paid a 15-25 percent commission on all sales that originate from their sites.

AUDIO TEXT PROGRAMS

Savvy adult webmasters looking for a way to supplement their income streams should consider participating in an audio text program, especially adult webmasters who cater to a well-defined niche market. Audio text is a generic communications term for information and entertainment services that are delivered by telephone. Sometimes referred to as "800" or "900" numbers, adult audiotext programs are organized along the same lines as affiliate and reseller programs. Under most programs the audiotext provider supplies and maintains the phone lines, hires the "actors", and keeps track of billing. Participating webmasters, on the other hand, concentrate on promoting the phone line and generating quality traffic. Webmasters receive a commission check at the end of every billing cycle based upon the total number of minutes billed to their line multiplied by their applicable per-minute rate.

In many cases, phone sex lines enjoy conversion ratios similar to pay site conversion ratios. Like with pay sites, audiotext conversion ratios are contingent upon the quality of the traffic sent to the line. It is not at all uncommon, however, for a well-promoted line to experience a conversion ratio often percent. Working with a top-of-the-line audiotext provider, such as *SinTalk* (www.sintalk.com) you can expect to earn approximately $1.50 for every minute of hold time. Hold time is the length of your surfer's call. A well-run program like *SinTalk's* will typically achieve hold times around ten minutes per call.

PAY SITES

Pay sites are not recommended for beginners. Pay sites are more time-consuming, resource-intensive and will not give you as quick a return on your effort as free and AVS sites. Our focus in this book is to make as much money as possible in as quick a time as possible with as less effort as possible.

Eventually, to reach the really big money in the high six figure range, you'll need to get in the pay site business unless you are a real whiz with traffic generation in which case you can stick with free and AVS sites.

Your money is made when the surfer becomes a member. You set your own prices based on what you believe is a fair market value for your content and on what it takes to entice the surfer to join your site. It's a classic pricing decision for a business.

Members pay using their credit card, an online check, a phone billing method or Pay Pal. You will not need to program your own software to be able to process payments, nor do you need to purchase any such software, as there are many third-party payment processing vendors that will provide this software for you and be able to get your site up- and-running in a matter of days.

Recurring Billing. Great profit potential with pay sites is derived from automatic recurring billing. Recurring billing allows you to automatically charge the credit cards of your members each month. This is also known as automatic rebilling.

The downside to recurring billing is that chargeback will be increased as a result. A chargeback is when a credit card holder disputes a charge and has his credit card company reverse the charge. This is bad for the Webmaster, not only because the money needs to be returned, but Visa, MasterCard, American Express and other credit card Holders limit the percentage of your sales that can be charged back. The penalty includes termination of your account.

Another great aspect of pay sites is that you can entice surfers with trial memberships. This greatly increases your sales conversion ratio of your traffic as people are more inclined to join with a trial.

Trial memberships include three or seven day trial periods either for free or a nominal fee like $1.95 or $2.95.

If you are compelled to start a pay site early in your entrepreneur career, be my guest. It may work out for you, but if it doesn't, it can be a lot of time and resources to find out if it doesn't work for you. For some people, it may be the way to go if you have intense interest in a particular niche or have another agenda such as using special skills you may have such as photography, graphics design or website design.

However, even if you really want to do a pay site, it is recommended that you start with free or AVS sites first.

The experience you gain with free or AVS sites will be invaluable for the creation and operation of a pay site. A lot of the basics of porn can be attained with a lot less effort.

The Proven Internet Business Models

A key to business success is to model what's already working. Most successful businesses have borrowed an existing idea and improved it or re-applied it in a new way. They don't re-invent the wheel.

To understand the various ways you can make money on the net, let's explore these Three Proven Internet Business Models.

CASSANDRA'S STORY

Cassandra is the mother of two daughters, one 17 year old and the other 25. She knows what it's like to miss out on a large chunk of the formative years of her children's lives.

From her background in management in a large collection agency to starting her own wholesaling business outside of the home in 1991—Cassandra was out of the house a lot as working mother.

After facing some pretty serious market changes in her wholesaling business, she and her husband finally decided to close down their 13,000 square foot ware-house.

This gave Cassandra the time to refocus and turn her attention to the home front. Although, her oldest daughter was out of the home and her youngest was already a junior in high school, Cassandra still saw tremendous value in being home for her family and only wished she'd gone into internet adult site business sooner.

She started in 1999, operating with AVS sites for 3 years before finally branching off into pay sites. She was content with her earnings from the various AVS with some income also coming from the commissions of various up sells, such as video sales as well as live video feeds and the various lingerie and sex toy retailers who were doing business at the time.

It's possible today to have a narrow specialization in revenue sources, but diversification has always and will always remain the best approach to absorb the bumps in the road that can transpire in the adult Internet business.

From annual income of $12,000, she quickly doubled to almost $25,000 in three months, and with the re-billing kicking in on her older memberships, she more than doubled even that amount to an annual $50,000 in the next three months.

After almost two years of working the adult Internet business, Cassandra figured that if she can earn $50,000 per year on a part-time Her potential earnings if she pursued her home business on a fulltime basis would be even more awesome. And considering the tremendous advantage of being able to give attention to her child at home she deduced that it was worth it to concentrate on being a fulltime work-at-home entrepreneur.

The big moves that Cassandra made when she worked fulltime on the adult Internet business involved creating two additional pay sites in different niche categories, and mainly, the extra time she was able to promote her sites through the search engines.

Cassandra felt she no longer needed AVS sites and concentrated only in creating and maintaining pay sites. It was simply an issue of personal preference. She relied primarily on her pay sites Niches she believed had good long-term potential. She created one pay site each for niches in big breasts, feet, BDSM, transsexuals, Asian female, and water sports.

Obtaining content for most of the niches was not difficult, as Cassandra relied on major wholesalers who packaged CD's of photo images on the niche categories that Cassandra specialized in. These CD's typically sold in the $150 to $200 range per CD, each containing around 300 to 400 images. For some lower quality filler content, Cassandra was able to purchase some CD's with over 1,000 images for the same price.

There has been no need for Cassandra to create her own original, exclusive photography to produce unique content. For her purposes, she has been able to get by, using nonexclusive content that is sold to other web sites.

Cassandra's content costs were at a minimum. She compiled an inventory of content that added up to $10,000 by that time-she was making $200,000 per year also; Cassandra leased video streaming content for her web sites, which cost her $3,000 per month. Of course, she did not incur this in the beginning, and this figure was expended when she made the $200,000 per year.

She had business car deductions as she took the liberty to splurge a little, with a new Mercedes Benz E320, and she also took legally allowable deductions on a number of business expenses.

Every year, she shells out up to $5,000 for a new computer upgrade and peripherals. She donates her older computers to family and friends.

Today Cassandra still maintains the same set of pay sites, and she's happily busy working the search engines, relying for the most part on free search engine listings, but now using paid advertising for some of the search engines.

Cassandra is a success story for work-at-home entrepreneur

I asked Cassandra if she wanted to share any secrets to success she gained from her years in business and she said, "Develop a niche, Keep up with the latest research and trends"

RYAN'S STORY

Let me introduce you to a pretty spectacular man, Ryan. He has impressed me with his determination and drive, I knew that I had to tell you all about him. Ryan used to be the owner of a printing business, which unfortunately folded. Four and a half years ago, Ryan was in need of a job. He was pretty good at surfing the net.... So, he figured he could make a business out of it. And he was right!

Taking a cue from a friend who was already an adult webmaster, Ryan decided to learn some HTML, ordered a $20 per month virtual server account and started creating quick thumbnail gallery pages for listings in the various thumbnail gallery post web sites on the Internet. Ryan created small thumbnail gallery pages, had them listed on the many thumbnail gallery post sites on the web, and capitalized on the massive traffic from some of the popular link lists.

A thumbnail gallery page is one page of HTML comprised of around a dozen thumbnail images each that clicks to a larger photo image. A page would have two or more banner and text links to sponsor web sites. A sponsor pays the Webmaster one of several ways:

A one-time upfront commission for each surfer who signs up in the sponsor's web site from the Webmaster's web site, back in 1999, sponsors paid typically in the $30 to $40 per signup range but rates varied to less than $30 and more than $40.

Recurring profit sales indefinitely in the future for each surfer who signup, for as long as the surfer remains a member.

A pay-per-click arrangement. Sponsors back then paid in the range of 5cents per click to 25 cents per click.

One-time upfront commission for the collection of surfer e-mails. The sponsor has a data entry form on a banner and pays the Webmaster a commission for each e-mail collected. A commission of 25 to 50 cents was typical.

Ryan was partial to sponsors who paid one-time up front commissions for each signup. Ryan used the thumbnail generator software called ThumbsPlus (company, CeriousSoftware at www.cerious.com), which he found very easy to learn and was able to gain proficiency in less than one free evening. With ThumbsPlus and Microsoft FrontPage to generate his HTML pages, a thumbnail page could be created in less than 5 minutes and quickly uploaded to the remote server of Ryan's web hosting virtual account.

But it hasn't all been smooth sailing. Ryan was frustrated early and it would have been understandable if he had quit the adult Internet business early. First, he learned quickly that a $20 per month web hosting virtual account could not accommodate the massive bandwidth required to make the thumbnail gallery approach a success. He found himself frequently exceeding daily bandwidth limits set by his web hosting company, which automatically disabled his account whenever that daily maximum limit was reached. The account would typically be disabled only hours after a web page would be listed in the thumbnail gallery post web sites.

Ryan was fortunate in that his web hosting company had the facility to disable an account when the daily bandwidth maximum is exceeded. A vast majority of web hosting companies do not automatically disable an account and instead allow the web pages to accumulate bandwidth for the whole month and finally send an outrageous monthly bill to the unsuspecting newbie.

Adult webmasters are generally not concern with the price of bandwidth/unit costs relative to their earnings. And compounding the problem is that there are many web-hosting companies that are not appropriate for high bandwidth activity and will charge an exorbitant rate.

The new Webmaster may be impressed that he or she is only paying $20 to receive a total of 1-gigabyte bandwidth allowance for the month and charged an overage of 25 cents for each additional 10-megabyte.

That may sound inexpensive.

That pricing above, or similar, is common among many web-hosting companies. Acknowledgeable Webmaster recognizes that a small-scale thumbnail gallery operation could require 1 gigabyte per day, or 30 gigabytes per month. Therefore, the above pricing would translate to a bill of $770 for the 30 gigabytes expended during the month. With 30 gigabytes per month, depending on your skill, you might be able to generate$400 in earnings, from say 10 signups that month. Well, you can see that you're already $370 in the red. Proceeding with Ryan's early experiences, he was fortunate to learn the lessons of bandwidth reality with a web hosting company that disabled his account and didn't allow him the opportunity to be zapped by an excessive bandwidth bill at the end of the month.

As we all know, nothing in life is free. These free hosts have requirements of the thumbnail gallery pages in that you as the Webmaster need to include a fair amount of the hosts' own banner and text links in the page. The downside to the free hosts is that your pages are overloaded with banners—yours and the host's. What that means is that the page load slower, thus eroding your surfer signup conversion potential, and more severely, surfers can be redirected to your hosts' banners instead of yours.

Nevertheless, Ryan was able to eke out some profits from the thumbnail gallery strategy in the neighborhood of $2,000 per month through the first half of 2000 using both his $100 per month virtual account with a web hosting company and free hosts.

During his first year of operation, Ryan was content to take his time and not rush his business. He frequented the many adult message boards and exchanged ideas with other webmasters he knew in the area.

One outcome of his discussions with other webmasters was that the importance of search engines finally began to sink in with him. Ryan quickly became an ace with search engines as he somehow had a knack for such work. Of course, a different revenue model was needed other than the thumbnail gallery approach.

In addition to the free sites, Ryan created a load of doorway pages that were directed both to his free sites and the pay sites of his sponsor companies.

As with the thumbnail gallery pages, the free mini-site contained banner and text links to sponsor sites. The sources of revenue for Ryan remained the same and he used the same sponsors as before, although he did experiment with a few others, which he eventually dropped. From the standpoint of sponsor selection, Ryan was fortunate to have a network of webmasters to rely on for advice. There have been a huge amount of fly-by-night outfits in the adult Internet sponsor community over the years.

Ryan ended up relying more on the free site strategy obtaining traffic from search engines although he did retain his operation with thumbnail gallery pages. He worked his way to earning $360,000 per year from all of his sponsors.

Today, Ryan's web sites are thriving. He credits search engines expertise for his success. About having an online business, Ryan says, "There are several things I like about working online, but probably the best is that I can set my own hours."

Setting his own hours has allowed him the time to completely remodel the house he is living in.

His number one tip for adult web masters running an online business is to set a schedule, but be flexible, "I try to have set hours for working...basically 9am to 5pm M-F."

JENNIFER'S STORY

When Jennifer gave birth to her first child three years ago, she knew she needed to find a way to stay home to watch her son grow and still contribute to the family income. She and her husband had just moved to Houston and Jennifer didn't like the idea of leaving her son at home to go out looking for a job.

Jennifer considered signing up for a pre-existing business opportunity and did some research into available opportunities. "Nothing seemed worth all of the hard work you put into a business," says Jennifer, "I couldn't find an existing business I could fall in love with."

Instead of joining a pre-established business opportunity, She decided to use her creativity to build her own businesses from scratch. She frequented chat rooms in 1999, particularly car enthusiast forums, and bumped across an individual who happened to be an adult Webmaster. Jennifer and the anonymous adult Webmaster ended up talking about business, which inevitably led to a discussion about the adult industry. Eventually, this led to Jennifer's start as an adult Webmaster.

Jennifer started off with the Validate AVS system. Within six months, she started one amateurish pay site, quickly added free trials and automatic rebilling and branched off and started four more pay sites, mainly mainstream porn with both soft-core and hardcore, an area which was more competitive than niche.

She worked the search engines like a lot of webmasters of that era and quickly gained expertise. In addition to the search—engines, Jennifer obtained arrangements with search engines and even Yahoo Europe for banner advertising. For contracted keywords, Jennifer's banners were positioned on top of the search engine pages whenever a surfer typed in those keywords for a search.

Banner advertising based on a per-impression cost has always been extremely risky and not for the faint-of-heart. In fact, it is very easy for a business to fall in a matter of days from the sheer weight of losses. A web site operator who uses this type of advertising needs two things: #1—to be extremely cognizant of his/her per-impression costs relative to his/her per-impression earnings, and, #2—have deep pockets.

Per-impression cost banner advertising is a tough game appropriate only for the select few. Banners need to be optimally designed to reach an even two percent click-through. If there are 100,000 impressions, a Webmaster needs to be extremely skilled, and lucky, to get 2,000 clicks. Most surfers don't even look at the banners.

With the 2,000 surfer clicks, and a good signup conversion ratio for most adult web sites of 2001, the numbers translate to 10 signups. That's 10 signups from 100,000 impressions. For most businesses, that's a horrible return. Jennifer navigated through the pitfalls of per-impression cost banner advertising. She fudged on the surfer visits by adding a plethora of exit console popup so that she could increase his signup conversion ratios. She tried to create entertaining content to extend membership retention as much as possible, and alas, she made it difficult for existing members to cancel—unethical in my book.

Within two years from his initial start, this enterprising fellow had contracted with major search engines for a monthly cost in excess of $200,000 per month. She reached Three million dollars revenue per year in two years since her quick start.

After a year and a half, she was down to zero in the net earnings department and bailed out as an adult Webmaster. She overextended her personal finances and quickly became accustomed to heavy spending and lavishes 30-day vacations.

Furthermore, her per-impression cost banner advertising was her own undoing. She signed contracts extending well into the future for the flaky Internet where there is much uncertainty about the future with regard to per-click earnings. Because of the rapidly changing competitive climate on the Internet, the per-click earnings formula from an earlier time became no longer applicable yet her per-click cost was fixed by contract.

In short, she was losing money from costly advertising. The fall of Jennifer is not surprising considering her lack of background on the basics of savings, investments and thriftiness.

Getting Started

Becoming a Webmaster seems like a simple decision. The reality is, it is extensive work requiring constant updating of knowledge. If you are interested in starting a web site and becoming a Webmaster, the information we provide below should put you on the right track. Here is the summery of topics you will be learning in the next few chapters.

WHAT IS THE WEB SITE ABOUT

Search the web and find out what you want to provide on your web site. Study your competition. Remember, it was Carl Segan who said, "It is every child's birthright to see the world anew". You have as good a chance as anyone to suceed on the web, but you need a plan. Once you know what your site is about and why it is unique, you need to determine; is it a free site? Will there be a pay area? Are you selling advertising? Figure out what your site is about and then move forward.

SITE LAYOUT AND DESIGN

As early as 1998, you could have simply slapped together an ill-designed page and still made money. Times have changed! Now you need Web Design that has site navigation. You need software like Microsoft FrontPage or Macromedia Dream weaver. An **HTML** WYSIWYG editor, (WYSIWYG is an acronym for "what you see is what you get"). Such as Microsoft's FrontPage or Adobe's PageMill or Macromedia Dream weaver conceals the markup and allows the Web page developer to think entirely in terms of how the content should appear. One of the trade-offs, however, is that an HTML WYSIWYG editor sometimes inserts the markup code it thinks is needed all on its own. Then, the developer has to know enough about the markup language to go back into the source code and clean it up.

HOSTING YOUR WEB SITE

There are millions of sites on the Internet and there are many offers for cheap hosting; use extreme caution! Some places will host your site for free if you put their banners on the top of your page and make your site look like theirs. If you want to make money, that is not the way to go! Professional companies that host adult sites tell you how many gigs you can transfer in a month for a specific price. Never, ever, use a host that promises you unlimited bandwidth. There is no such thing. Essentially what they are betting upon is that your site will not be successful. If it is, you will hear "you exceeded the bandwidth amount we allow". Always remember, there are no free lunches; bandwidth costs money. Fees are passed on to you as service charges. The Professional web hosting services you select will probably be the most important decision you will make. One other point worth noting...Never use a web provider that also handles your credit card processing. If you ever decide to change Hosts, it will be very difficult since they will be controlling the scripts that provide the credit card transactions. There are many options for you to choose when it comes to Merchant Services.

GETTING THE CONTENT/DATA

Once you know the concept of your site (theme) you will need pictures or video, or other data, which will interest those who visit your site. Some sites can be profitable if you have a digital camera and a few open-minded, wild or kinky friends. Many sites are simply girls who chat LIVE with others using Live Webcams. Other sites depend on visitor submission via e-mail for their content. We strongly suggest that you visit the Content Providers for unique licensed and copyrighted material. NEVER use under-age models. There is a difference between Adult Material and material that is not only illegal, but also immoral. We all know where that ultimate line is drawn and staying on the safe side of the line will allow you to remain profitable and out of the legal web.

NAME YOUR SITE

If you want the name of your site to match your domain name, then you have to search the registry to see if the name exists. Do not get discouraged if you cannot easily find a domain name you like. There are thousands of domains for sale. It would initially seem like every sexually oriented combination of words has already been registered, but that is not really the case. Keep trying and be original.

CREDIT CARD SOLUTIONS

Selecting the right credit card solution for your website is one of the more important decisions you will make. You cannot use your regular bank to processes your membership payments since they all require low-risk purchases such as buying a product from a store. Adult sites cannot swipe a credit card and therefore the charge-back rates tend to be high and are therefore considered high-risk by the banks. Any attempt to use your local bank to process credit cards without their knowledge of exactly how you are using it will have you quickly terminated by the bank's merchant processor, leaving you with no solution and basically dead in the water. There are a few well-known high-risk solutions.

ADVERTISING YOUR WEB SITE

Promoting your site is the key to success. List your site with the adult search engines and think about Newsgroups and other available Advertising Programs. The more places you get the name of your site listed, the more traffic you will get. CAUTION: When you spend substantial dollars on major search engine advertising, MAKE SURE you are totally confident in your web host provider. You are going to get a lot of traffic…If your site is not performing FAST under heavy load, you will literally be throwing out your money since visitors to your site, during heavy peak hours, will not get your web page to their screens. Most free web hosting or low-cost web hosting cannot assure you of high-traffic performance. When you spend tens-of-thousands of dollars on banner advertising, you cannot stop it just because your site is not about to handle the load. Select your Web Hosting carefully.

PROTECTING YOURSELF LEGALLY

Now that you have spent time, effort, and money to create your web site, you need to protect your intellectual property. Since you created it, it's your property and nobody has the right to use it without your permission. Also, since you're in the Adult business which serves many different areas of the country, areas with different criteria of what constitutes obscenity, you need to not only protect your intellectual property, you also NEED to protect yourself. The major players in this industry all have full time legal staffs, but even through you're a small businessperson you shouldn't go without legal coverage or legal insurance. Many very affordable legal plans are available for the home-based and small businessperson. Like auto, life, home, and medical insurance, you really need to be covered with legal insurance too, especially in this business. With the advent of low cost high quality legal plans, legal coverage is a must have for the small business owner.

Essential Hardware and Software for Adult Webmaster.

Why Webmaster need to know what's under the hood.

Computers are like cars—as long as they work, we don't care to understand what happens technically inside. This is an unfortunate attitude that many users share, but the reality is that you don't need to be a rocket scientist to service a modern computing system.

HARDWARE

The essential computer hardware components include:

A powerful personal computer Computers running either the Windows or Macintosh operating system is acceptable. Windows-based machines should be powered by Pentium microprocessors, while Macintosh machines should contain the Power PC, or G3 processor.

Lots of RAM (random access memory) A basic rule is to buy as much RAM as you can afford. We recommend 512 Megabyte.

A large hard disk Once again, buy the biggest hard drive you can afford. We recommend minimum 40 gigabyte 8000 rpm.

A high-resolution color monitor driven by a 24-bit color card You need a good monitor so that you can position images accurately. Make sure the monitor's image is clearly set because you will be staring at it for hours at a time. The 24-bit color card is important if you plan to work with color images; it will allow your monitor to display nearly 17 million colors.

A modem With a modem you can send files to and receive files from remote locations customer, service provider, writer, artist, word-processing operator, or any one of the many people with whom you might work.

Connections to the Internet Clients increasingly expect to send and receive files via the Internet. If you have a modem, you can easily connect to the Internet using various web browsers and electronic mail packages.

Unfortunately, even the fastest modems are too slow to effectively deliver large graphic files. You may wish to install direct Internet access using lines separate from your telephone.

SOFTWARE

The hardware listed above will do absolutely nothing unless appropriate software is installed on the computer. Electronic prepress technicians usually have several pieces of software available:

An up-to-date operating system Most application require A Macintosh to be running System 7.1 or later, a Power Macintosh to be running System 7.1.2 or later, and a PC machine to be running Windows 98, Windows 2K or Windows XP.

A program to manipulate images Sometimes photographs and other graphic images to be used in a Web Page document need to be altered. Image editing programs, such as Adobe Photoshop or Macromedia Fireworks, can manipulate photographic images.

What is your web site about?

This Chapter will help you Plan the WHAT, WHO, AND WHY of Your Web Site

- What is your web site about?

- Who are your target audience?

- Why would they want to look at your web site!

NICHE

A "niche" is just any specialty area or focus that a site wants to concentrate on, in order to target the market interested in that content. A niche may be so broad as to hardly deserve the name (e.g. hardcore or soft core), medium-specific (e.g. Asian or mature), or start to get quite precise, as in the case of most fetish sites. Niches are a way of addressing a particular market of surfers, and thus compete with the ocean of other sites out there.

WHAT IS A MICRO-NICHE?

It's a niche so fine-tuned that it's an actual rare possibility that anyone else in the world has your niche listed anywhere else. How do you know you've gone too far, too deep? When you can't find a sponsor that would work well with what you've created. For example, if you can't find a photo of an 18+ Asian model with blonde hair wearing a cheerleader outfit sporting pigtails and a bullwhip—then you're in trouble. Chances are if the photo doesn't exist—then a pay site that caters to this super micro niche won't exist either.

You've gotten your audience targeted; all wet and ready with anticipation and then BAM—you send them off to a sponsor that can't take them the rest of the way. If you send them to "Site XXX" that features dark-haired Asians in cheerleader outfits sporting pigtails and a bullwhip, you've "almost" got what they want—but are missing an important element. And if this is what they've got to offer on the outside—forget them being happy on the inside.

WHAT IS FETISH?

The American Heritage Dictionary of the English Language (Fourth Edition, 2000) gives four senses of the term "fetish:"

1. An object that is believed to have magical or spiritual powers, especially such an object associated with animistic or shamanistic religious practices.

2. An object of unreasonably excessive attention or reverence: made a fetish of punctuality.

3. Something, such as a material object or a nonsexual part of the body, that arouses sexual desire and may become necessary for sexual gratification. 4. An abnormally obsessive preoccupation or attachment; a fixation.

The last three senses are the ones of interest here, giving two criteria for regarding a niche as "fetish:"

An abnormal or excessive preoccupation Gets off on object or non-sexual body part

That's a little clearer, but still leaves a fair amount of wiggle-room, from two sources. First, there is leeway in both criteria-"excessive" and "abnormal" are open to interpretation and "gets off" can run from just occasional fun foreplay, to always absolutely necessary. Second, both these criteria apply to the market, which is broader than just true-blue kinks-it may include the curious, casual, intermittent, regular part-time, and full-time interested parties. But, fetish niches are different from garden-variety niches.

WHAT ARE THE ADVANTAGES OF A NICHE SITE?

A main advantage of hosting a niche site is that there are many hardcore, softcore or babe sites on the Internet and garnering traffic to a new one of these standardized sites is a tremendous uphill battle. A niche site is capable of reaching surfers looking for unique content and has the possibility to stand out from other general-purpose porn sites.

Along with reaching specified customers, the niche site works well as a venue to sell niche sponsor programs and memberships. Just as general-purpose sites are everywhere, so are general-purpose sponsorships. You get a better chance of getting your work seen when you choose to make a niche page.

Niches are also as numerous as their fans. There are so many fetish and off-center porn lovers and they have varied tastes. You don't have to settle for promoting the same old straight, tired porn when you can promote unique and wanted content.

WHAT ARE THE DISADVANTAGES OF A NICHE SITE?

You might not like what you see. When you go into the niche world, you will learn there is content that you may not like looking at. Remember that you have to promote legal content. Only choose a niche you feel is comfortable and safe for marketing.

The silver lining to the above disadvantage is that what is considered niche in the adult Internet may not be what you think. For instance, legs and pictures of them is a niche. Images of nude women smoking cigarettes are a very popular niche. Good old-fashioned nipples are a niche. There are far more explicit fetishes and their lovers. The kinkier the fetish, the better the market. The crux being that a niche site can be a surer path to your Adult Internet success.

Like it's murky definition of specialized market, the adult Niche site can be indefinable. What exactly is a Niche? Is it a fetish? Is it a body part? Are gay sites niche sites? Is Babe content a niche or a general type porn site? In the following sections, we will delineate different niches, what sponsors can be used for them, how to acquire content for them and how to market them effectively.

WHAT ARE SOME NICHES?

Here are the niches for you to consider. Select one or two that you are comfortable withand for which you easily secure content (this is discussed later in the book). Although Entrepreneur is strictly a basis and you would treat the images and other content as merely data, some people may simply be turned off by the though of dealing with a foot Fetish site, for example.

AMATEUR

There's been a lot of attention directed toward the world of adult amateur lately. Webmasters try desperately to get a piece of the amateur action

Some of the most prominent companies in our industry built their business on a foundation of Amateur porn. The adult Webmaster that deals in Amateur can expect a ready-made audience and an abundance of ways to profit from this favored niche.

What can you do with Amateur content? Pretty much anything you want. You can build a free site or a pay site. You can build a TGP, a link-list site or just gallery. You can promote older Amateurs or coed Amateurs. You can market gay Amateurs or tranny Amateurs. There's Amateur bondage, interracial Amateurs as well as exotic Amateurs. Amateur models can be gorgeous, average, or downright homely. There are BBW Amateurs as well as Amateurs with tiny tits or petite frames.

If you want to buy Amateur content, there's tons of it available for practically peanuts. If you want to shoot your own or invest in exclusive content, you can.

Whether you need static images, video, live feeds or plugins, you will find plenty of content producers that deal in the Amateur niche.

BIG BEAUTIFUL WOMEN (BBW)

BBWs (acronym for "**B**ig **B**eautiful **W**oman") are the focus of a vaguely-defined, fairly widespread Internet subculture with interests centered around the acceptance, support, and admiration of larger women. Generally defined as an attractive, self-confident "woman of size", the BBW is the subject of much veneration by so-called fat admirers (FA). Admirers may also be referred to as "chubby chasers", although this term is more frequently used to describe gay men who seek larger men.

The BBW niche is widely misunderstood by a vast majority of adult webmasters, especially those who sell it but don't 'get it'. If one categorization of adult entertainment demands an understanding of its audience it would be the BBW category. No matter how unpleasant in appearance you may find a BBW model to be your audience thinks her soft flesh and supple folds are exquisite. BBW means "Big Beautiful Women". Don't forget the 'beautiful' part.

Even among lovers of BBW, there are differences of opinion about what is big and how much is too big. A model with twenty extra pounds in this rail thin/fake boob culture doesn't fit well into either babe or BBW. Plenty of men find a meaty gal to be very sexy but she's marketed more efficiently as an amateur model than she would be as a BBW model. A BBW model cannot be merely chunky. She must be large.

CELEBRITIES

Celebrity sites are those, which feature actors, actresses, singers, athletes, politicians, aristocrats and other people in the public eye. They are often peek-a-boo voyeuristic type of pictures obtained by paparazzi or clips of nudity extracted from movies.

ETHNIC: ASIAN

Ever since the beginnings of Taoism in China and Tantra in India, the inhabitants of the Asian continent have had a more sensual outlook on sex than their western continental counterparts. The Chinese, Indians and Arabs all were polygamous cultures who promoted sex as an expansion of the spirit. These countries/cultures produced religious and nearly religious texts devoted to the perfection of the sexual act.

You can make a site that covers the map of Asia totally or concentrate on hotties from specific countries. You could include Asian sponsor banners on sites that feature International cuties.

While some fetishists might like their models or dominatrix to look Asian, Asian content is niche content and should not be confused with fetishism. Whatever you choose, learn as much about the Asian niche as you can. Get to know your surfers and do your best to provide them their true desires.

ETHNIC: BLACK/EBONY

The Ebony niche means the models are black. They can be females alone or males alone. They can be two women or two men or male and female, but the fact that the models are black is what categorizes the imagery as ebony.

Ebony can be a stand-alone theme for a free-site or paysite or it can be mixed in with other niches. For instance, a site that centers on teen content could incorporate ebony teen models. A gay site could have an ebony section. Mature content can be blended with ebony models of the same age range. Even a kitchen-sink, general porn site benefits from ebony content. Perhaps the only themes that might not work well with ebony would be bondage or fetish pages, but this isn't a stone-etched rule.

Ebony content is fresh and sexy. It's got a definite following and customers willing to pay money to access it. Whether your intended market is gay, straight, male or female, you will find that adding ebony to your collection of images and video will garner you a whole, new source of income.

ETHNIC: HISPANIC

Latina means a woman. A Latino is a man. This content is popular and profitable for adult webmasters. Major adult sponsors offer at least one Latina site to promote in conjunction with their programs.

Adult content providers seem to have no trouble finding beautiful and sexy Latina/Latino models. There's Latina teen content, Latino gay content, Latina MILF content and Latin interracial content. There are feeds and adult classifieds that incorporate Latina into their programs. From softcore bikini stuff to full on gangbang, whatever kind of porn you want to sell, you can find it done with Latina/ Hispanic performers.

If hot, Latin models are your thing, then enjoy your work and sell what you like. Hispanics are the largest minority group in the US alone. The lust for this gorgeous ethic group is forever. Just like any sex, Latina/Hispanic sex sells!

INTERRACIAL

Whether the content is hardcore, softcore gay or lesbian, if the images involve two or more people of different races, it can be considered interracial content.

Interracial porn has a well-proven market performance among interested purveyors. Some may love seeing video and photos of Asian women giving a blowjob to a white man. Others may like the look of a Latina getting gang-banged by a group of black guys.

An Interracial site can be a free site, a paysite even an AVS. You can make great gallery money by submitting interracial gay or straight galleries with sponsor links to interracial paysites. You could make your own paysite or Top List or Interracial TGP. There's even a market for stories containing interracial sex.

Interracial content can be as simple as two cheerleaders of different ethnicity jumping together to as extreme as black transsexuals having anal marathons with businessmen. If you choose to promote or build an interracial gallery or site, you will find you have a steady audience and plenty of ways to make money from them.

EXHIBITIONIST

Voyeurs get their kicks from viewing others surreptitiously. Exhibitionists want to share their glory with the universe. As the exhibitionist craves exposure, the exhibitionist content lover craves the content. Technically, all adult models are exhibitionists. But when it comes to content, there are certain guidelines one should follow when looking for exhibitionist imagery.

For content to be considered as exhibitionist it must contain models who pose in public or outdoor settings. The true thrill of sexual exhibitionism comes from getting caught. Whether on the street, in the park or in an office filled with shocked workers, the exhibition lover gets off on exposure.

Like most niches, the exhibitionist niche can be applied to any type of adult site. One can run a free site, a top list or a paysite featuring an exhibitionist theme. Also like most niches, it might be difficult to find exhibition content.

FETISH—ACTION SPORTS

This category refers to an interest in athletic women, whether merely posing in various stages of undress in their athletic attire, or involved in various sports activities.

This niche category may even be broken down into specific sports. There are niche sites that provide content only in one sport: tennis, wrestling, boxing, weightlifting, and catfights.

A word about cat fighting. That is not an established, recognized sport like tennis or boxing. That is more of a contrived sport for the entertainment of male customers in which women are pitted against each other for the fantasy of a no-holds-barred combat.

Fetish—BDSM

BDSM means Bondage/Sadomasochism. Actually, it means so much more than any text can describe. The two men from whom the terms Sadist and Masochist originate, were both authors that wrote endless tomes about the more extreme side of sex.

Leopold von Sacher-Masoch wrote a book about his favorite fantasy titled "Venus in Furs". Women who beat him while wearing furs sexually aroused him. Masoch became masochism. The Marquis De Sade wrote about the pleasures of dominating and inflicting pain on a sexual partner. While no one has ever proved that the Marquis actually participated in such activities nevertheless, De Sade became sadism.

Not to be confused with fetishism, which is a sexual attraction to inanimate objects or body parts, BDSM lovers can also be fetishists. BDSM fans can be married, straight, gay or even celibate. Their interest's cross-sexual identity and you will find such a mix at the many BDSM gatherings and clubs already in existence.

The current western culture frowns on BDSM but such was not always the case. Submissive/Dominant examples of sex in the name of religion can be traced back as far as recorded history.

Building a BDSM site means that you will be appealing to more than 25 percent of the world's population. Bondage people are very private and because of social taboos, have to conceal their activities to public. That is one reason why the adult Internet is the perfect market for the BDSM clientele. The web allows S & M admirer's privacy and freedom. The Sadomasochist fancier is a very profitable and faithful niche.

FETISH—BESTIALITY

Bestiality fetish is a sexual fantasy involving any type of animals. Avoid the bestiality fetish for your selected niche. *It is illegal in the US.*

In fact, any site that you create should never contain any representations of bestiality.

While you may reside in a country where bestiality is not illegal, remember that much of the Internet, including web hosts, sponsors and other web resources, reside in the United States, where this category is illegal.

FETISH—BREASTS

Breasts. Knockers. Jugs. Ta ta's. The breast lover niche seems to be self-explanatory. Anyone can make the connection, but the allure of this niche is more than the obvious.

When a breast lover sees a hardcore penetration photo, the role the breasts play is the turn-on. Most women have two breasts but there are twenty times two types of breasts to love. The tit niche even has sub-categories like big tits.

Obtaining content for big tit sites is an easy effort. Models (who will not pose for more graphic images) pose for breast shots happily. Whether you want your breast site to feature high-rez or amateur images, you can find hundreds of CD and ZIP files with the big boobs you want.

Your big boob site could be themed to feature natural breasts, or only abnormally huge tits. Make you site appear to be a club of big knockered housewives or present it as the collection of a fellow big jug freak. As long as the breast pictures are big, the big tit lover will come.

Fetish Ass/Butt

An ass site can be on a pay host or a free host. An ass site can have a hostess or can be themed almost any way you want. You can use really rude language on a butt site or promote it as softcore. You can feature anal pictures or sponsors or even promote boob lover's content along with your ass content. Ebony content and sponsors work nicely with ass content. Upskirt and panty sites work well with a butt site.

Perhaps the most popular ass-type niche these days is the Big Booty niche. Thanks to celebrities like J-Lo and Beyonce, there is an abundance of fans that love a round, firm backside. Hip-Hop music videos further encourage the niche. Whether your goal is ass fucking or ass worship, the butt niche is a good niche. The sky is literally the limit for an ass page.

Fetish—Feet

There are several derivations of foot love. Some like the appearance of the foot. Some like the smell. Others are not attracted to the foot, but rather are turned on by the shoe. While one may like to tickle a foot, or have their genitalia caressed by feet, others would rather kiss the foot or simply admire the way a foot looks in a pair of sandals.

To run a foot fetish site the Webmaster must understand that foot lovers look at the feet in the same ways the others look at breasts and butts.

You can take your own photographs of feet but you had still better make sure your models are of legal age and that you have them sign waivers. The best way to make sure that you get proper foot content is to purchase it from professional content vendors. These people fully understand what appeals to the foot lover and take the appropriate photos.

FETISH—GOTHIC

Goth was an offshoot of punk that delineated the darker more melodic music of Bauhaus from the thrash histrionics of the Sex Pistols. Later Goth generations incorporated Victorian Gothic themes and lore into the culture, which explains the vampire connection. Novels such as Anne Rice's "Interview With a Vampire" became more than just popular reading among Goths. Many of them fancied the vampiric lifestyle and blended in with the S&M community.

Goth content can be gay or straight, bisexual or asexual. One can collect Goth galleries on a straight TGP or add Goth content into a Feminist porn site. Goth can fit in a lot of places and is an up-and-coming niche for adult webmasters.

To advertise Goth content, one must obtain it. Goth content already has its share of affiliate sponsor programs and content providers.

Goth adult content can be extremely graphic playing to the vampire/bloodletting fanciers. It can be relatively tame reminding the surfer more of Betty Page than Marilyn Manson. Goth content can be glamorous and glossy or it can be grainy and look like amateurs submitted it. Goth culture has community and can work in congruity with adult personals and chat rooms. Goth may be just the niche for you.

FETISH—LINGERIE

The appeal of pantyhose and stockings needs little explanation. They envelop the leg and enclose the foot. They thinly veil the nether regions. Their manufacture employs thousands of people and generates income for millions of resellers.

A Webmaster can build a whole web around a hose theme with categories such as ripped hose, hosed feet, panties under nude hose and models in garters and stockings. Adult site builders can add hosiery pics and videos to the categories on their fetish sites. A softcore babe site can relegate a listing for babes in stockings to their collection of glamorous models.

You'll find surfers who prefer stockings and others who cannot get enough of seeing chicks in their all over panty hose. The foot fetishist might also be into legs and the filmy stretches of nylon that covers them. Hose shots can fit in almost anywhere on the adult Internet and it's pretty hard to go wrong using pantyhose content.

If you are interested in the hosiery niche, you're interested in a niche that has a good following and has the potential to make you money.

FETISH—MIDGETS

As the niche name suggests, this is a niche having to do with a fantasy interest in midgets. These can be soft-core or hardcore sites, and typically are both.

Midgets may be engaged with each other of similar size or with normally dimensioned people of both genders.

FETISH—PREGNANT AND LACTATING

Women who are pregnant are very alluring. So alluring in fact, they have their own porn niche. The swollen bellies and engorged breasts are an incredible turn on to many lovers. Pregnant women are more alive, more female and they obviously like sex. They can't get pregnant and their breasts produce a refreshing drink. Oh, and they glow.

An adult Webmaster that works with pregnant content has many site building possibilities. One can make a free, pay or AVS site featuring pregnant content. One can have a model as a host, or claim husbands and boyfriends send in the content and call it an amateur preggo slut site. A Webmaster could design a pregnant TGP or top list. You could even make decent money by just building pregnant and lactating thumbnail galleries and submitting them for listing. Even selling other types of programs such as fertility herbs or sex toys would work well with pregnant content.

Whether you want to build a free site, paysite or TGP with pregnant content, you will probably want to incorporate affiliate-coded banners to sponsor programs. There are sponsors that include pregnant models within their fetish programs and there are sponsors that feature sites that are exclusively pregnant.

FETISH—SMOKING

Smoking content and smoking sites have been around since almost the beginning of the adult Internet. Maybe viewers like the oral aspect of smoking content. Maybe it's the taboo quality of smoking in today's society. Whatever the reason smokes and smut have been a winning combination for many an adult Webmaster.

While there is some smoking content, which is hardcore, smoke stuff is primarily softcore content. Most often smoking content involves a single model in various stages of undress. The thrill comes not from an actual sexual act but rather from the model smoking. In fact, there is quite a lot of smoking content where the model isn't nude at all. The excitement comes from the cigarette between two pretty fingers or from the puffs or from the foggy exhale. Smoking the cigarette is the sex act to a lover of this niche.

If you ran a TGP or a top list, you would include smoking images in one of your categories. You could build a whole free or paysite around a smoking theme but like with any niche, your audience will be limited.

Smoking content is fairly easy to find. Models are much more likely to suck on a cancer stick than they are to suck on a penis. If you like to market gay content, there's even smoking stuff just for your audience.

FETISH—UNIFORMS

Uniform love is a fetish almost anyone can understand. Uniforms symbolize so much. Discipline, service, bravery and power. The doctor with a white coat and stethoscope. The fireman with a big hat and sharp axe. The policeman with the shiny badge and long nightstick. That lady sergeant with her tailored suit and tight, little hairdo. Everybody looks sexier when they're wearing a uniform.

The adult Webmaster has a lot of choices when it comes to uniform porn. There are plenty of sponsors and content for almost any configuration of uniform sex site. Perky cheerleaders, hardhat hunks, smoldering soldiers and nurses galore! Build a free site. Build an AVS or paysite. Go for the gay audience or select the straight market. Lure in the Goth and BDSM crowd with rubber/latex uniform drag. Fulfill a lonely housewife with stories of sex and the pizza boy.

FETISH—WATERSPORTS

To the uninitiated, this niche name may connote sports activities that are practiced in the pool, river or beach. Rest assured, though, that the subject is an entirely different matter. It involves urination.

There is a sexual fantasy by some people to observe images and videos of models urinating in different situations. The models may urinate in public or in the privacy of the bathroom. The fetish may involve solo urination and any combination of group urination.

In fact, the urination in a group setting may also include urination on each other.

Other names for these types of sites are "peeing", "pissing", and "golden showers" sites.

TRAMPLING

Trampling is sexual pleasure derived from being stepped on. Sometimes the person likes the thrill of feeling a high heel on their genitals. Sometimes the trample lover gets off on the pressure of being stepped on. There are trampling fetishists that like bare feet on them.

Like with many fetishes, trampling fans are usually highly educated men who use trampling to come to terms with their feelings of guilt about oppression of women in a male dominated world.

Gay men are also trampling fans. Trampling is many times featured on BDSM or Bondage/Domination/Sado Masochist sites.

Trampling content by itself is very hard to find. It is most times sold in conjunction with shoe fetish and BDSM images.
A dominatrix type hostess would be good theme for your trampling content and sponsors.

MATURE

The mature niche is a good niche. Many find girls between the ages of 18-21 to be uninteresting and undesirable. They prefer that to see women of experience and substance. They want women who not only show their bodies, but also look as if they might actually have had sex. Some find the mature model brings back memories of that sexy mom down the street or that math teacher with the tight skirt. Even others get good and hot looking at women who literally remind them of sweet sweet grandma.

These discerning individuals are also more likely to shell out money to Mature model paysites. The world is saturated with young, pore less teens. Mature women (thanks to Madison Avenue) are hard to find. The mature niche is a solid, productive moneymaker.

ANIME AND HENTAI

Cartoons have always been popular and pornographic cartoons have a definite audience of fans. Drawn characters don't have to supply proof of age documents. They don't have to be paid and they will do anything their creator wants. Cartoon content is so popular, it even has it's own categories.

One of these categories is Japanese cartooning called Anime. You can recognize Hentai/Anime by the impossibly big eyes and small mouths of the characters. For all those who look for real-life porn, there are as loyal, smaller groups who look for this toonish content. They visit free sites, take paysite tours and look at galleries on TGPs. You can reach them in as many ways. They are more net-savvy customers.

To keep your anime content legal and above board, you can purchase it or acquire it by affiliating with a sponsor. This way, you can be sure you have product that is licensed by its creator's and deemed for an adult market.

THE GAY NICHE

Gay porn is one of those categories of adult online sex that shouldn't really be considered a niche. Like straight, hardcore, softcore or teen, the gay niche has a huge and regular following. A Webmaster can make an extremely good living depending on only gay content. By that same virtue, there are so many successful gay paysites that a new adult Webmaster might face formidable competition. They might find themselves having to incorporate gay sub-niche content or sponsors to make sure they get as much opportunity to make money as possible.

The majority of adult content providers sell gay images and videos. There are even gay-specific content providers. You can buy image sets and video clips or streams. You can get hardcore or softcore content. The difference with gay content as far as hardcore/softcore is that softcore involves solo models or no genital contact between male models. Oral or anal sex is hardcore.

Whether you open a free or pay gay site, you will probably use sponsor affiliation as a means of earning income. AVS, TGPs and gay top list sites can benefit from gay referrer codes on their pages. There are tons of gay sponsorship programs.

REDHEADS BLONDES AND BRUNETTES

Put three men in a room and show them a video of three different girls with three different hair colors and you'll probably find that at least one of them will favor the redhead over the blonde. You might even get a three-way split of preferences where one fellow will dig on the brunette. A site that features models that all have a certain hair color are extremely popular niche pages for the adult Internet.

You'll have no problem finding content and sponsors for hair color niche sites. The haircolor niche is not a new one. What will be new is your theme.

You could launch a haircolor-based Thumbnail Gallery Post. You could put images of a hot redhead behind the protection of an AVS ID. You could open a paysite that features only blonde gay males. Your site could be a softcore gallery free site that is categorized by haircolor models. Then you would make money by offering more hardcore content from the haircolor sponsor banners you display. You could even go farther into the niche and build brunettes in bondage site or something along those lines. You could create a lesbian site and link all your models by hair color.

If you have a free site, AVS site or want to make additional income from your pay site, then you are in luck because there are numerous hair color affiliate programs for adult pages. You can offer your surfers more hardcore content or full-length videos at the paysites of you sponsors.

BALLOONS

The idea of sexual gratification from balloons has probably been around for a long. Perhaps it's the balloon's roundness or its feel when inflated. Whatever it is, there are a great many people on this planet who have a fetish for balloons.

They call themselves looners. They love images of sexy models posing nude and semi-nude, sitting on big balloons, straddling them, squeezing smaller ones between their legs or stroking their bodies with them. Some loonists love video of perky girls popping balloons, while the popping turns others off.

To add balloon imagery to your adult site, you will need balloon content. If you shoot your own, you might find your legal-aged models more compliant to do the work, as it is a fairly harmless fetish.

If you want to use balloon love as a way to make money in the adult Internet, you'll want to try some of the sponsor affiliate programs where you make money by selling memberships to paysites. There are a good amount of sponsors with balloon fetish sites to promote.

PLAIN AND SIMPLE GIRLS

Beauty is relative.

Ours is not to question why surfers get turned on by things that mystify us. Our job is to sell the surfer what they want and there are a large number of smut searchers who like plain girls.

There are fans of every body type and age in this world. They have sexual desire and they have money and to ignore them is to ignore an incredible source of Internet porn income. One niche that sells well is the Plain Girl niche.

A person can build a whole adult site that has a plain girl theme. The site can be set up so that it appears to be hosted by a plain girl who shares imagery of her and her friends. It could have a theme as if some guy has a thing for plain girls and wants to share his collection of them on video and in pictures. A plain model site can mix hardcore images with softcore solo shots. Plain model content could be grouped with amateur and older model content.

BABE

The Babe can be a young man but most times the Babe is a young woman. Babes are not teens. Babes are not blossoming. They are wholly grown and in their full womanhood. Babes are more attractive, more perfect, more like a dirty beauty queen.

A site can include Babes as added filler or they can build a whole network of Babe paysites. Babes can be the central theme with chat and voyeur cams and personalized email newsletters. A TGP site can be a Babe TGP with Babe galleries of different ethnicities, different outfits and different hair colors. Babes content can be incorporated as special free content for a more text-based magazine adult site.

FOOD CONTENT

Food is on the ground floor of the pyramid of life. Air water and food, these are the things humans need to live. Without them, the human cannot move up the pyramid to the next level, which is sex/procreation. Food is basic. Taste is one of our senses. A good meal can be positively orgiastic. Food and sex are closely linked. Our first experiences with intimacy concern food. For some food is sex. To them food means sex and sex is not sex without food.

You can add food pictures as a garnish to your hardcore, fetish or softcore site. You can build all your menus into one grand banquet for Insertion lovers. Trampling and foot fanciers dig on nutrition pulverization and incorporation. Food appeals to men, women, straights and gays. Food is erotic, exotic and comfortably familiar at same time.

You can utilize food as the content for your free site or Top List or as member's content for your paying customers. If you want food to be a pivotal topic for your AVS site or TGP or gallery then the addition of food-centric sponsors can greatly enhance your fiscal undertakings

MILF NICHE

MILF stands for "Moms I'd Love to F**k".

The older niche is a popular one but it is more far reaching than MILF. This very specific fantasy was made popular by the movie "American Pie". The general mature niche includes old hookers and even older grandmas. It doesn't have the babe factor MILF does. The models shouldn't be runway quality but they should have a certain lusciousness. An MILF can be white, African American, Asian or Hispanic. The MILF model just needs to remind the surfer of the inviting, good smelling Lady down the street that gave him a hard on.

You can do a lot to make money with this new and popular adult niche. There are several affiliate sponsors who will let you market their MILF paysites. MILF content has begun to appear in product listings of adult content sites. Marketing MILF content is less risky because fans of MILF prefer women over 21. You can sell this niche with a free site or by the gallery. If there isn't an MILF Thumbnail Gallery Post, there will be. MILF content can be mixed with ads for adult classified and dating services. MILF is a self-sustaining commodity. MILF is set apart from ordinary older/mature content.

TATTOOS AND BODY PIERCING

Twenty years ago, western fashion would have never presented a tattooed model in any layout or ad. You would only find a nose piercing on a punk. Now a person under 35 is almost odd if they don't have a body part pierced or tattooed.

Even the bodies of once pristine high-fashion models sport the erotically placed belly ring or ankle tattoo. There are large communities of body modification fans from the moderate to the extreme. They have magazines, trade shows, websites and fans planet-wide. Let the lovers of unadorned physiques have their fun. You can sell to devotees of piercing and tattoos.

As you can see, there's more pierced/tattooed content available than there are sponsor sites specifically geared toward the market. No worries. You can take pierced/tattoo content and build a free site or TGP around it. You can link pierced/tattoo content with fetish, BDSM and Goth sponsors. You can get your own tattoo/pierced content and create your own paysite. Just because there aren't tons of paysites aren't out there doesn't mean the audience isn't.

REALITY

One of the historically strongest niches on the adult web has been the amateur niche. Much to the chagrin of shallow folk, surfers have clamored for ordinary-looking models. Porn searchers find content and buy memberships to thousands of amateur paysites each day. The amateur niche disproved past attitudes about film quality and model perfection. The rise of the amateur niche gave rise to the reality niche.

Since reality content can be defined with such a broad brush, it's important to delineate between reality content and amateur/voyeur. Reality content possesses the traits of a documentary done smut style. Reality sites are produced and portrayed as actual encounters, filmed as they are happening. Reality content appears to be unscripted and unrehearsed.

At the moment reality content is a fairly easy sell. The right keywords in your META tags and appropriate content on your pages should get you the audience you desire. You can make a free site, paysite, TGP or top list. You can make your reality site hardcore, softcore extreme, gay or straight.

TRANSSEXUALS

The transsexual is more than a person of a sex, adorned in the clothes of another. The transsexual is no illusionist. The transsexual goes through an actual physical transformation. In the adult Internet, the transsexual niche is a very popular niche. There are hundreds and hundreds of thriving "tranny" sites both free and pay. There are tranny sponsor programs and tranny TGPs. There are content providers who specialize in shooting transsexual models. If you're looking for a profitable niche, you can't find one with more promise than the transsexual niche.

It's hard to define the exact reason why the tranny niche is so hot. Part of its popularity is due to curiosity. Another part is due to the fact that a lot of folks are turned on by trannies. Men are visual creatures and there's no vision more mind-blowing than a beautiful woman who used to be a man. Transsexuals are a phenomenon almost as new as the Internet itself. Back when the web belonged to a few universities and the DOD, there were only a handful of transsexuals in the world. Now there are millions of people surfing the net and there tens of thousands of transsexuals living on the planet.

Any type of site can be a tranny site. You can build a paysite, a free site, a link list or a TGP. There's that much available to the adult Webmaster. There are quite a few content makers to shop from and a good number of sponsor programs for you to promote. Most TGPs include a tranny category for submission, as do most top lists. If you know your audience and market effectively, you can make a living in the transsexual niche just as you would in the straight or gay end of the adult Internet.

BIG PENIS / MONSTER PENIS

While it's natural to assume that women and gay men would be your target audience for the monster cock niche, think again. Everybody loves a big dick, even heterosexual males. Naturally women and gay men love a big cock but there are quite a few heterosexual men who enjoy watching images and video of monster cocks inserting themselves in assorted orifices.

Monster cock content can be used on almost any type of adult site, be they free or pay. However, this is hard-to-find stuff. The big guys are few and far between. Just because a man's got a monster cock, that doesn't mean he wants to share it with the adult Internet.

As said, big dick content appeals to a number of markets. The safest bet—when it comes to actually making profits—would be to build a big cock site that appeals to gay men. Women may love the cock and they may be the ones who spend the most money on the web but the fact remains, women statistically don't buy adult paysite memberships. Of course you can gear your huge penis site to a straight male audience but it would be best to use it within a collection of different types of niche content.

You could definitely use big dick images and video clips as gallery filler. Monster cock stuff would also work well as an addition to your existing content. By nature, the penis is considered to be hardcore. Nevertheless one can use single male model stuff quite effectively when marketing to true lovers of the big gun.

GROUP SEX / ORGIES

Basically, when you think of group sex/orgy content in the Webmaster vernacular, think of multiple couples and triples and such. Gangs-bangs and three-ways are sort of group sex/orgy content, but not exactly.

Group sex/orgy content can be either softcore or hardcore. Among adult webmasters, hardcore involves actual insertion shots. A male model can assume the positions without actually doing the deed. In other words, like most adult content, softcore is more hocus-pocus. So if your orgy imagery is comprised of graphic insertions and thrusts and goo, it's hardcore. If the content shows no such stuff, it's softcore, orgy or not.

When it comes to finding group sex/orgy content, you're probably going to find more softcore than hardcore. Group shoots are hard to choreograph and the addition of actual sex makes the creation even more difficult. Not to mention, it costs more to hire that many performers. Just the same, the niche is out there and readily available to purchase from content providers.

The adult affiliate can benefit financially through effective marketing of group/orgy sponsors. As with all sponsor/affiliate programs, follow the rules and listen to the advice of your chosen sponsor.

Group/orgy content is available but might cost more. Adult affiliates can make sponsor money by promoting group/orgy sites. Group sex/orgy content is yet another Cozy way to keep you in the green!

LESBIANS

If you're interested in promoting the Lesbian niche, you are not alone. Everybody loves Lesbians!

Straight men love them because they just do. Straight women love them because lesbians don't appear to be exploiting each other. Lesbians love lesbians because they're lesbians. Even some gay men enjoy watching a little carpet munching from time to time.

Content producers have very little trouble talking models into a lesbian shoot. Women usually aren't afraid to touch each other, even when they're naked. There's practically no exchange of bodily fluid in a lesbian scene. This is a safety factor that is very appealing to the female model. Lesbian shoots are usually happy and light-hearted. If there were such a thing as non-threatening, inoffensive porn, it would be lesbian porn.

The Webmaster that sells the lesbian niche will find a myriad of venues from which to market their wares. One can create an entirely lesbian-based site or one can tuck a bit of lesbian content in with other niches. Got a babe site? There's room for some lesbian babes. Got a bondage site? Then add some lesbian bondage. Got an interracial site? Don't forget the interracial lesbians.

Right now, lesbian porn is at the height of fashion. It's almost chic to be a lesbian. That might change some day but there will always be an audience for the ladies who munch.

What is HTML?

HTML stands for **HyperText Markup Language** and is the main programming language that makes the Web.

Background HTML codes lurk behind all zillions of web pages on the Net. Many pros actually build web pages or at least fine-tune them by typing in and editing HTML codes directly. If you don't want to do that, fortunately, you don't have to.

Microsoft Word, for example, lets you save your documents as HTML-based web pages. This way of working is called **WYSIWYG** (**W**hat **Y**ou **S**ee **I**s **W**hat **Y**ou **G**et)…You design a document on screen so it looks like what you want. The program you're using then generates the necessary HTML codes to create a web page that a web browser such as Netscape Navigator or Internet Explorer can display.

The WYSIWYG HTML editors allow beginners to build complex web pages by simply "dragging and dropping" onto the work area. These programs eliminate the need to learn HTML, so you can concentrate on the look of your page.
But if you are serious about doing more than a page or two, it's to your benefit to learn HTML basics, because these programs generate too much extraneous code and it's often necessary to "tweak" it manually. That's why many pros think that the best web pages should be hand-constructed.

HOW TO LEARN HTML

The basics are quite simple. HTML files are plain text files with special "tags" or HTML codes that a web browser knows how to interpret and display on your screen.

Here is the link if you want to learn HTML

http://www.w3schools.com/default.asp

FRONT PAGE

When it comes to Web authoring tools, none is as simple to use at Microsoft FrontPage. With its generous amount of wizards and it's library of templates and images, it's a beginner's dream. You won't need a large staff to create a site that's both useful and professional.

Primarily people who would consider themselves beginner HTML editors use Microsoft FrontPage. If you have a need for professional HTML editing, you should find a professional HTML web developer. However, you probably don't need this kind of assistance, because it is reserved for websites that need more technical requirements like 128-bit encryption.

If you have a web page that you use for home or small-business purposes, learning FrontPage will greatly help you. It will enable you to create web pages and maintain them. This will solidify your presence in the online world, and provide your customers with an online information source about your business.

In the age of the Internet, learning FrontPage is now more important than ever. Microsoft FrontPage is a program that creates and edits the Hypertext Markup Language, or HTML. It is the code that web pages are made of, so it is used billions of times all over the Internet. Its relative simplicity and easy learning curve has been the reason for HTML's worldwide success

The advantage to learning FrontPage is that it is used in conjunction with other Microsoft programs, including Microsoft Word and Microsoft Excel. If you need multimedia capabilities in your web pages, FrontPage is a good program to use because you can import other file types into FrontPage with relative ease. This includes Word documents and Excel spreadsheets

MACROMEDIA DREAMWEAVER

Available in both Windows and Macintosh platforms, Macromedia's Dreamweaver is a powerful and popular WYSIWYG Web page builder that allows the user visual design capability, as well as direct access to HTML code, at an affordable price. A Macromedia product, Dreamweaver enjoys the reputation of Macromedia's tools among professional designers. Dreamweaver has a Quick Tag Editor that allows swift modification of tags, defined for a given selection, without leaving the design view, while NetObjects allows the easy insertion of content from Flash and Shockwave.

Dreamweaver also allows advanced users to re-format the code from HTML files created in Word 97, 98 and 2000, as well as import pre-formatted data from spreadsheets into Dreamweaver HTML tables. It's very hard to go wrong on a Macromedia design product, and Dreamweaver is further testimony to the excellence of the Macromedia design suite.

DREAMWEAVER VS FRONTPAGE

1. FrontPage as all Microsoft product has so many templates and ready to use solutions that you cannot admit it is easier for beginner to start using FrontPage to build his first website. You can create simple website personal or business with several clicks and all you will need to do next is to enter your text and pictures instead of used by FrontPage by default.

2. The good news is FrontPage html pages look exactly as they appear in MS Explorer and the bad news is that they look perfect ONLY in MS Explorer. However you may program FrontPage to get rid of nasty tags but I believe it requires some hand coding to adjust pages to Netscape or Opera. Another good news for FrontPage users: about 93% of all Internet clients use MS Explorer 5 and higher.

3. As Microsoft application FrontPage is better with ASP pages, which are standard for Windows based hosting and windows based programming.

4. MS FrontPage perfectly interacts with other MS Office products. For example you can easily cut and paste some chart from MS Excel into FrontPage working area.

5. By default MS FrontPage uses table with the fixed width and sometimes it can be a problem to make it display tables with percentage width.

PLUSES AND MINUSES OF MACROMEDIA DREAMWEAVER:

1. You can build your own templates and use them to edit hundreds of pages of your website with one single click. Although Dreamweaver adds some comment tags to html file to distinguish editable and non-editable areas and I read in one forum that people experience some troubles applying template to more then 700 pages as they ran out of memory but I had never chance to test that.

2. Pages done with Dreamweaver usually have less trash in coding. They look almost perfect with Netscape, Opera and MS Explorer.

3. Dreamweaver doing amazing thing with SSI files and other server side include technology. Php code looks much nicer however with ASP scripts FrontPage still better.

4. Dreamweaver is much better interacts with other macromedia products.

5. Both editors in most cases display CSS (Cascading Style Sheets) correctly. But if you enter style attribute twice in Dreamweaver for it will definitely ruin your page and you will be able preview your page partly before this error. FrontPage however handles such mistakes easily.

My idea is that MS FrontPage is ideal for beginners as it provides so much help and templates, then you should move to Dreamweaver when you feel yourself more comfortable with the html.

GRAPHIC SOFTWARE

ImageForge from CursorArts Co.

ImageForge is a freeware image editor with painting and editing tools. Allows you to import images from scanners and digital cameras, apply special effects filters, and create photo albums and slideshows. Other features include zoom, crop, enlarge canvas, resize, resample, rotate, replace colors, smudge, scatter, clone, natural tools, gradients and patterns, automatic palette optimization, and more.

If you can't afford to purchase software, you can still find free software to create and edit images. Some of this software is developed by individuals, and some is feature limited or an earlier version of a more advanced program. In some rare instances, there are no strings attached, but most often you will need to provide information to the company by registering, or endure ads or "nag" screens.

http://www.cursorarts.com/

GIMP for Windows

GIMP is a popular open-source image editor originally developed for Unix/Linux. Often lauded as the "free Photoshop," it does have an interface and features similar to Photoshop. Because it's volunteer-developed beta software, stability and frequency of updates could be an issue; however, many happy users report using GIMP for Windows without significant problems. It doesn't support GIF format.

http://www.gimp.org/windows/

Serif PhotoPlus

Serif has long been giving away previous versions of their software to entice users to purchase the current version. Currently you can download a completely free, fully-functional version of PhotoPlus 5.5, or order a CD and pay only shipping costs. PhotoPlus 5.5 features an export optimizer, editable text, image slicing and image maps, selection tools, smart shapes, and image enhancement tools.

http://www.freeserifsoftware.com/

Pixia

This is the English version of a popular free painting and retouching software that originated in Japan. It features custom brush tips, multiple layers, masking, vector—and bitmap-based drawing tools, color, tone, and lighting adjustments, and multiple undo/redo. Like many freeware editors, there is no support for saving GIF format. Also available for many other languages.

http://park18.wakwak.com/~pixia/

Ultimate Paint

Ultimate Paint is available in both shareware and freeware versions for image creation, viewing, and manipulation. It has been designed to be fast and compact, and if you're familiar with the old Deluxe Paint program from Electronic Arts, Ultimate Paint is said to be very similar. The freeware version is an older release of the full-featured shareware product.

http://www.ultimatepaint.com/

PhotoFiltre

Although it's fairly limited in features, PhotoFiltre offers a simple, but elegant user interface and a lot of one-click image adjustments, filters, and effects. There is a built in image explorer panel for visually navigating your file system, basic drawing, painting, retouching and selection tools, and batch processing capabilities. Unfortunately, without layers or transparency support, it's not very useful for much more than playing around with filters and simple adjustments.

http://www.photofiltre.com/

VCW VicMan's Photo Editor

This award-winning graphic editor offers a variety of painting and editing tools and features including a text tool, gradients, selections by color or region, color replacement, editing in any scale, special effects and so on. This free version is an enticement to upgrade to the Pro version for $29.95 US, so you can expect to put up with nag screens.

http://www.vicman.net/vcwphoto/

ImageForge

ImageForge is a freeware image editor with painting and editing tools. Allows you to import images from scanners and digital cameras, apply special effects filters, and create photo albums and slideshows. Although this is teaser program for the shareware ImageForge PRO, it's probably a few steps above Microsoft Paint.

http://www.cursorarts.com/ca_imffw.html

Before you read this book any further, you should decide what HTML editor and Graphic Software you want to use. Install the HTML editor and Graphic Software into your PC or Mac and start practicing. Here are the links to useful links:

Microsoft FrontPage

http://microsoft.com/frontpage

http://www.accessfp.net/

http://www.anyfrontpage.com

http://www.intranetjournal.com/articles/200003/fp_index.html

http://www.frontpageworld.com

Macromedia Dreamweaver

http://www.macromedia.com/software/dreamweaver

http://webdesign.about.com/cs/dreamweavertips

http://www.andrewwooldridge.com/dreamweaver

http://www.dwfaq.com

http://www.dreamweaverfever.com

http://www.dreamweaversites.com

HTML

http://www.htmlgoodies.com/primers/basics.html

http://kirkhamgate.net/webbeginner/first.html

http://www.w3schools.com/default.asp

http://www.hwg.org

http://www.weijers.net/guide

http://www.vrwebdesign.org/HTML

http://www.websiteprimer.com

http://www.w3.org/MarkUp

http://www.w3schools.com/html/html_reference.asp

http://www.htmlhelp.com/reference/html40

http://cedesign.net

http://www.htmlclinic.com

http://www.htmlgoodies.com

Graphic Software

http://www.cerious.com

http://www.photodex.com

http://www.esmarttools.com/ThumbnailBuilder/index.htm

http://www.raizlabs.com/software/magic/

http://www.onfocus.com/snap/index.asp

http://www.linkup.dk/gallery/

http://www.stgsys.com/stgthumb.asp

Choosing a Web Host

One of the first decisions that to make when building a new site is where and how it will be hosted. Typically, you will have four choices when deciding what type of hosting service you need:

FREE SERVICES

Many first-time adult webmasters start with free hosting packages. Free hosting services generally offer the most basic of hosting packages, offering a limited amount of disk space to store a Web site in exchange for displaying an advertisement on your site promoting their service or an affiliate's service. While a free hosting service isn't the most versatile option, it is definitely a good start for someone who is new to the Internet's adult industry and wants to learn more about the details of site building and administration.

HOW DO THE FREE WEB HOSTS MAKE MONEY?

The free hosts often make money in other ways, such as putting banners, popups, or popunders on your site. Some free web hosting companies do not put ads on your site, but require you as the Webmaster to click on banners in their control panel or signup process, or just display banners in the file manager in hopes you will click them. Some lure visitors with free hosting in hopes you will upgrade and pay for advanced features. A few send you occasional emails with ads, or may even sell your email address. A new method that is becoming popular is requiring a certain number of "quality" forums posting, usually as a means of getting free content and displaying more ads.

ARE FREE WEB HOSTS RELIABLE?

Generally no, although there may be a few exceptions. If the host is making money from banner ads or other revenue sources directly from the free hosting, then they likely will stay in business, provided someone doesn't abuse their hosting with spam, hacking, etc., as often happens to new free web hosting companies with liberal signup policies. If the host accepts just anyone, especially with an automated instant activation and it offers features such as PHP or CGI, then some users invariably try to find ways to abuse it which can cause the host to have a lot of downtime or the server to be slow. It is best if you choose a very selective free host, which only accepts quality sites (assuming you have one).

USES FOR FREE WEBSPACE

Free web hosting is not recommended for businesses unless you can get domain hosting from an ad-free host that is very selective. Other reasons for using free hosting would be to learn the basics of website hosting, have a personal website with pictures of your family or whatever, a doorway page to another website of yours, or to try scripts you have written on different hosting environments

HOW TO FIND THE RIGHT FREE WEB HOSTING

The best place to search for free webhosting is on a free webspace directory website (i.e. a site which specializes in listing only free web hosting providers). There are some which add new free hosts pretty much every week (and if it is updated often, has usually had to delete about as many). There are also many, which almost never update their site, and a huge percent of their links and info are outdated. Unfortunately that includes most of the directories that were the best several years ago. The problem is free hosts change so often, and most fold up in less than a year (often even after only a day or two), that it is hard to keep such a directory up-to-date.

Hints for finding the best free web hosting Generally it is best not to choose a free hosting package with more features than you need, and also check to see if the company somehow receives revenue from the free hosting itself to keep it in business. As already mentioned, it is best to try to get accepted to a more selective free host if possible. Look at other sites hosted there to see what kind of ads are on your site, and the server speed (keep in mind newer hosts will be faster at first). Read the Terms of Service (TOS) and host features to make sure it has enough bandwidth for your site, large webspace and file size limit, and any scripting options you might need. Read free webspace reviews and ratings by other users on free hosting directories. If you don't have your own domain name, you might want to use a free URL forwarding service so you can change your site's host if needed.

SHARED SERVICES

Shared hosting services are the default option for most hosting companies. If dedicated or co-located services are not explicitly ordered, chances are you have purchased a shared server. Shared hosting means your site is being stored on the same server as a number of other Web sites. Unlike many free services, most shared hosting packages allow you to have your own domain name and up to 10-15 email addresses and aliases. Larger sites, however, likely won't be able to take advantage of the cost efficiency of shared hosting, as most limit the amount of bandwidth available to your site, and offer smaller amounts of space.

DEDICATED SERVICES

Choosing a dedicated hosting package is a must for sites that have a large number of images, plan to offer any type of e-commerce or intend to attract large volumes of traffic. Companies offering dedicated hosting packages will provide your site with its own server that share a machine with anyone else. Although more expensive than a shared package, dedicating hosting is a must for larger adult sites, as the packages typically offer the most space and bandwidth.

CO-LOCATED SERVICES

If you're apprehensive about leaving your hosting in the hands of another company, but don't have the funds to physically maintain a server and direct Internet connection out of your home or office, a co-located server is the next best thing. With co-located servers, a hosting company will connect your hardware to the Internet and provide you with rack space, a secure environment to store your server in, and technical support. What you are responsible for providing is the actual server, maintenance and software. Co-located servers generally give you more control over your hardware without having to worry about vandalism, theft or connectivity.

BANDWIDTH

Put simply, the bandwidth is a measure of how quickly data can be sent through a circuit. It's usually measured in bits per second (bps). The larger the bandwidth of a line, the quicker it can transfer data. Think of a beach-bound, two-lane highway: day-to-day traffic flows just dandy, but on a heat-waved Labor Day weekend? Forget it—that quaint highway's a parking lot. But if the highway were replaced with an 8-lane freeway, you'd have the sand between your toes in no time. When it comes to bandwidth, a T3 is that 8-lane highway: It's about thirty times as fast as a T1 line, which is 50 times as fast as a 28.8 modem, which is twice as fast as a 14.4 (the two-lane highway). Though just because you're sitting at the end of a blazing T3 doesn't mean you're at the beach yet. You may be able to receive data like lightning, but if the info's being dished up via a meager connection on the server end, you still have to sit and wait for it just like everybody else.

THE LINES: T1, T3, DS3, OC3

You should gain a good knowledge of these labels! Many of us don't know the real meaning and consequently don't understand which one of these available lines would better suit our needs. In the adult entertainment business it's easy to see that the size and the amount of data (transmitted/received) changes according the bulk of traffic. The above labels (T1, T3, DS3, OC3) are just names used to describe a certain amount of data transmitted at once. You can think about it as a pipe, and web pages and data as water. The wider the pipe is, the more water you will be able to send through at once: or the better the line is, the more information (text, web pages, video, images, audio) you will be able to send at once! For most websites it comes down to how many people are looking at the page at once (during the busiest time of day) and how much information they are getting from the page.

T1 (1.5 Mbps)—This line is able to transmit about 17 gigabytes per day. Let's imagine an adult oriented site with just a few graphics, for example 20 pictures, spread over 4-5 pages with some text. It would take roughly a visitation level of 40,000 people per day to have that site transferring that much data per day.

T3 (45 Mbps)—This line is equal to about 30 T1s.

DS3 (45 Mbps)—This line is the digital version of a T3. These lines can be presented over copper, coax, or optical fiber.

OC3 (155 Mbps)—In layman's terms, a shit-load of bandwidth. Digital, presented over optical fiber.

Most of you for sure won't need anything close to an OC3 line, but it's good to know about labels so that your web hosting company when they try to strike you with big words doesn't hypnotize you! Well it isn't so important what kind of pipe they have as long as they don't try to put too much water trough it (too many clients/web pages on it).

The second piece of the puzzle for choosing web hosting is what hardware they are putting your pages on. If they provide to you with something that is similar to a desktop computer, then it doesn't really matter how big the pipe is…the computer will get slower and slower trying to send out your pages. Consequently another question could be: "What kind of servers are you running and how much load level do you allow on them?" They could lie here, but you may be able to check up on this. Take a look at their client list, and if they tell you they have 5 Pentium 155s and the list has like 200 clients that are mostly adult sites, you can imagine they either they lied about their clients or you are going to be on a really slow server. Also you need to find out what type of operating system the server is using. UNIX based operating systems are good for supporting heavy traffic like that of adult entertainment sites.

The last piece of the puzzle is the routing equipment you are going to use (routers, hubs, etc.). To use the water analogy you can think about routers and hubs as on the ends of the pipe. If the pipe is 6 inches in diameter but the fitting on the end only opens to 3 inches, then you can't use the whole pipe. The chain is only as good as the weakest link and the routing equipment is the link between the lines and the servers. So, be sure to ask your future web-hosting provider what kind of equipment they have. I don't have tons of info on brands and what I print here would get outdated too quickly anyway. Just remember that there are 3 primary pieces: lines, servers, and routing equipment.

WEB HOST ACCOUNT

http://www.cozyfrog.com/

http://www.xbiz.com/articlearchive.php

http://adultcheck.com

http://charlie.ynotmasters.com/

http://netmechanic.com

http://hostreview.com

The Importance of Content

Unfortunately, many webmasters and business owners overlook the true value of quality content in today's competitive business market. In "the old days," as veterans love to go on about, webmasters would merely slap up scanned images from men's magazines, take still shots from film media or use badly photographed amateur images to fill up the virtual pages of their electronic storefronts. Eventually people realized what they were doing was actually illegal, and content companies were born, providing CDs full of images for webmasters to use on their sites. Plug-in feeds, downloadable movies and other forms of content were soon to follow, but the content industry within the adult online industry, had a slow and small beginning at first too—not unlike any other demographic within the business.

Debates—or board "pisses," depending upon your point of view—would be waged on industry forums for years to come, discussing which was more important—quality or quantity. The popular affiliate program sites of the time focused more on the quantity factor, and it soon became a numbers contest with banners boasting hundreds of thousands of images, videos, erotic stories and other mediums of adult-oriented content. Finding content wasn't the problem by this stage of the game, but finding "quality" content—now that was the trick.

Quality content was available, as was "exclusive content"—but of course it was offered at a price. Quality soon became the distinction between a successful pay-site and a floundering one. Eventually, as the market became more and more saturated and content businesses began offering more options, niches and began focusing on shooting more quality images, content became more affordable and the average website began to look better for it.

Today's Webmaster has literally thousands—maybe even hundreds of thousands—of options in the current content market. Just about anything you could ever want, need or hope for can be found at an array of affordable prices, exclusivity options and/or quantities. Fortunately, the industry has moved well beyond the days of simply scanning images from magazines…unfortunately, our collective respect for content itself is still sorely lacking, as many webmasters simply do not understand the weight of its importance.

CHEAP CONTENT

You may have heard that the best things in life are free—but that's not necessarily so in the world of adult content. While legal, quality content doesn't always mean that you will be shelling out a ton of money, you have to realize that free content doesn't always mean it's even going to be worth that free price tag. The most important thing you need to remember when purchasing content for use on the Web is the license—getting a legal license that allows you to utilize the content in the manner necessary to achieve your goals is vitally important.

The downside of cheaper—or even free-for-use content is that it quickly becomes over-saturated within the market. More expensive content packages—based upon quality, rarity of the niche and/or exclusivity rights—will be less saturated within the market and will of course be more valuable to you and your site. Cheaper content is excellent for TGPs, link sites and sponsor program promotions—especially if you can grab the content as soon as possible once it is released for use. Once it has become over-used in the market, even the TGP and link list managers will begin denying your sites, as they will demand something not so overdone.

Free and cheap content can be compared to other industry freebies like free hosting or free graphic/logo design. It's a great way to get started, get your feet wet and find your way around building websites. However, if you are building a pay site or other professional industry program, you will want to make sure that your membership and design are worth the money that your members pay. A crappy site will only hold their attention for so long—and crappy, over-used and overexposed content will increase your chargebacks and threaten the survival of your business.

QUALITY CONTENT

High-Quality content is what we would all like to have—if we could afford it. However, as we have discussed, it should be used specifically where necessary—in your tours, in your members' areas and in your niche-specific, targeted advertising. Remember, it's all about sales and retention…getting the surfer interested enough to click, holding that interest and deepening it until he wants to join your membership site—and then continuing to keep that customer happy so that he renews his membership with your paysite for months to come.

Quality is of course—as is beauty—in the eye of the beholder, but should always be in high resolution and professionally photographed. Your best bet for high-quality content sources is to get recommendations from other webmasters and paysite owners. It's always a good idea to comparison shop as many content providers and brokers as you can find, just to make sure you are getting exactly what you are looking for.

EXCLUSIVE CONTENT

There are several "levels" of exclusivity—and of course all of those levels come with a varied degree of pricing. Again, deciding what is needed for your site will be an individual decision based upon your target audience, niche and membership needs.

100% Exclusive—This means that NO ONE else will have rights to these images except for you. Expect to pay TOP dollar for 100% exclusive images…Many site owners may choose to hire their own photographers and/or video teams in order to obtain purely exclusive content, especially when a specific look, niche or theme is needed.

Semi-Exclusive—This type of content is generally limited to a specific number of clients for purchase, say five to a dozen—with some even extending to twenty or more. Again, this depends upon the provider or broker, and price will be affected depending upon how many other sets/copies of this content will be made available to other site owners.

Limited Exclusive—A timed exclusivity—sometimes giving you anything from a couple of weeks to months of 100% or semi-exclusive use of the images. Price will vary from dealer to dealer, but a limited exclusive deal can be great for webmasters who add fresh content on a regular basis and only need to have exclusive rights for a specific amount of time.

LEGAL USE OF CONTENT

This is where things can get tricky. The advice I've always given over the years—and still give to this day—is that all webmasters, and especially adult paysite and/or affiliate program owners, should hire legal counsel. The industry has been buzzing about changes to the US 2257 content regulations all year long and whenever there is a lot of discussion, there is usually a lot of confusion. Having an experienced industry attorney on retainer to check your sites, double-check your 2257 content record-keeping and make sure that the content you are using is LEGAL can be worth its cost hundreds of times over. Adult websites are still legal in the US and the only people getting arrested at the moment are site owners that do illegal things…not paying taxes, not keeping legal content records, using sneaky tactics, etc. You should hire an attorney not just for checking your content and reviewing your sites, but also to ensure that you are doing everything in your power to run a legal business.

With regard to legal use of your purchased content, you will need to check the license that you are given by the content provider, photographer or broker that you purchase your content from. Some packages allow you full use of the images—to be used in your banner advertising, logos, site tours and/or printable materials. Other packages state clearly that the images can be used on your website only and must not be cut, changed, altered or otherwise manipulated for alternative use. Make sure to ask questions BEFORE you buy—and read, re-read or even ask your attorney to take a look at your license before you do anything you are unsure of.

Of course other things need to be considered before you just go out and buy some content to slap up on your website. Having an attorney reviewing things should avoid problems overall, but making sure that the content you are purchasing is legal in YOUR area is something everyone needs to consider. Some countries have different age restrictions on models—some need to be 18, some can be younger or are required to be older. Some places have restrictions on animal sex (think Mexican donkey bar content) and/or specific niches and fetishes (consider extreme BDSM type stuff). Use common sense and seek professional counsel and advice—remember "I didn't know" doesn't hold up well in court.

BUYING THE **RIGHT** CONTENT

And finally we come to probably the most important aspect of purchasing content…buying the RIGHT content for your site. If you are promoting a gay site, you probably don't want to purchase straight couple sex images—no matter HOW hot the guy in the photos happens to be. And if you are promoting mature housewife content, your models will need to be just a tad older than 20-something.

It all comes down to knowing your niche, your traffic and ultimately your members. Knowing what they want, what they are looking for—and what keeps them coming back for more—can be the difference between an OK site and an over-the-top popular site with thousands of regular, recurring members!

Doing the research—taking the time to ensure that you are getting the right niche, right type of content (broadband versus dial-up speed video), the right quality of images and even the quantity necessary to keep your customers happy—is more important than most webmasters realize. If an adult site were a sandwich, content would be the meat of that sandwich. You can fill it all up with cheeses, top it with flavorful condiments but ultimately when people order a sandwich; they name it by the meat ingredient. When surfers want a blonde college babe site—they want to see some blonde college babes. When someone signs up to a hardcore fetish site—you'd better offer a lot more than just some hotties dressed in leather.

Hiring a Web consultant, a niche expert or other knowledgeable advisor can save you a ton of money by preventing you from buying the wrong content for your core audience—and can help you to see profits from your new venture possibly earlier than you'd even expected. We've all seen sites, programs and businesses that just "click."…Sites that pop…images that seem to have just been "made" for the niche or theme—and designs/layouts that just bring it all home. Making sure you do it right from the very beginning is what separates a winning business from a doomed one. Don't make the mistake that hundreds of webmasters make every year, and make sure that you take the time to do the work, conduct the research or listen to your hired niche consultant.

The most important thing that I hope you will take away from this article is to remember that finding content that is the right quality, niche, exclusivity and format for what you are doing should be a top concern for anyone designing or working with paysites. Getting new members, keeping current members happy and carving a true niche for your self with a highly targeted quality website should be everyone's goal. Get the right content at the right price for your site—and don't, even for a moment, settle for second best.

FINDING CONTENT

http://www.web-legal.com

http://www.adultlegal.com

http://allsexinone.com

http://www.exclusivecontent.com

http://www.freshphotos.com

http://www.bestadultcontent.com

http://www.cdbabes.com

http://www.scarlett.net

http://www.sweeterotica.com

http://www.fetishbrokers.com

http://www.xamo.com

http://www.xxxcontentdirect.com

Selecting Your Domain Name

Selecting a domain name can be a very frustrating process as a lot of domains have been sold already. With 30.000+ domain names being sold each day it can be a challenge to find the appropriate domain name for your company. So what do you do? Your business name might not be available or be too long. If you did think about doing business on the Web when you started, your name might not be appropriate for the web. What if your domain name is available for the country code extension but not .COM? Should you buy the .NET anyway? How long is too long?

Create a short list of domain names and variances. Talk with people that you trust and opinion you value. However, don't wait too long about as 30.000 Domain Names are being sold a day now. Below you will find a few pointers or things you should have in mind when selecting your Domain Name.

Using your business name or Niche as your domain name could be a great idea. However if your business name is really long or very complicated you might want to consider searching for an abbreviation or an alternative.

Recognizable you want it to reflect what you do…that makes it easier for people to remember your address and will increase the chance of people guessing your web address right without having to search for it.

UNIQUENESS

Choosing a Domain name that is unique can avoid that you loose business to your competitors, as it cannot be confused with other domain names. You still have to consider if the Domain name is easy to type and not too complicated. Most unique Domain Names for .COM are gone and a lot have been bought to re-sell a lot more expensive. If you have a look on eBay you will see a lot of Domain names for sale.

A person had already registered the Domain name for Pope Benedict XVI before they announced the new Pontiffs name and had put it for sale on eBay immediately after the announcement. He sold it for $200.000+. Think carefully about buying your domain name from another person. First of all you would have to pay a lot more than registering a new name. Second, you might not have full ownership of it.

Maybe find alternatives as the one for sale by a person might never be sold and then end up being available through a Domain Registrar a couple of years down the road.

EASY TO TYPE

You should select a domain name that is easy to type so avoid complicated domain names. You would like people to be able to enter your Web Address very easily. Spelling errors might make them end up at the wrong site. Or if your domain name contains a hyphen "-" and your competitors domain name has none. They might end up there instead.

WHERE IN THE WORLD ARE YOUR CUSTOMERS?

Should you choose a Country Code Domain like .CA or .US or .IN or just buy a .COM or .NET? As the domains are selling very quickly now for the .COM then people start to use the Country Code domains more. Clients and potential customers are getting more computer/internet savvy and as businesses are starting to use the Country Code domains more, they will catch on to that quickly.

MULTIPLE DOMAIN NAMES

If you are a business in US that expect to have clients all over the world you might want to consider selecting your domain with both .US and .COM extension. How this would work is that your main web site could be your .COM address but if people type in your .US address they are automatically forwarded to your .COM address. You have to ask for your .US to be forwarded to the .COM address. It's that simple and with the low prices on domain names not a big expense. Another advantage is that if you have a unique domain name you can avoid someone else reaping the benefits of your advertising. People still tries to enter Web Address with a .COM first so if you had bought the .US address and someone buys the exact name using .COM they would open your competitors web site first.

Like any brand name, logo, or trademark, your domain name represents part of your business identity. Customers will associate it with your particular product, service, or business—if you name it correctly. Remember that you domain name will probably be used for several purposes, including your site, email address, and possibly an ftp or other server. It will be a part of your overall business marketing campaign.

If your domain name can be easily remembered then you will attract more customers. People will use your web site or email address to get immediate and convenient access to the information or service that you are providing.

In addition, domain names are portable. You can move physical address, change phone numbers, change Internet service providers, change the company that hosts your web site, and still keep the same domain name

RESERVE YOUR DOMAIN NAME YOURSELF

You can do this even before you select your web hosting company.

Register your domain name with the registrar of your choice YOURSELF! Do not let your web hosting company do this for you.

If you let your web hosting company do the registration on your behalf, there is a good chance they'll sell your name and email to data bank companies.

To avoid that likelihood, you should register the domain yourself. You should select a registrar, who is likely independent from your selected web hosting company.

DOMAIN

http://www.icann.org/registrars/accredited-list.html

http://www.nsiregistry.org/whois

http://www.bulkregister.com

http://www.networksolutions.com

Merchant Accounts

WHAT IS AN INTERNET MERCHANT ACCOUNT?

For a merchant to be able to accept credit cards for payment on the Internet, the merchant must have Internet merchant accounts for each type of credit card he wishes to accept online. The merchant can obtain Internet Merchant Accounts from an acquiring institution, such as a bank. The acquirer authorizes the purchases made with the card and ensures that the funds are deposited into the merchant's bank account. Soltrus and VeriSign act as the channel for moving the credit card transaction from the merchant's web site to the acquirer's processing network, receiving the results, and posting them back to the merchant's site. VeriSign also facilitates the settlement of funds from the cardholder to the acquiring institution.

There are five main components or players in the credit card processing system. They are (1)the credit card issuing bank, (2)the consumer, (3)the merchant services account, (4)the acquiring processor/acquiring bank, and (5)the merchant bank. The credit card processing system has been carefully set up to insure that all parties involved will be able to take advantage of this efficient way of doing business. The credit card authorization process is basically the same whether your business actually swipes the credit card through the credit card terminal, keys in the credit card on the pad of the credit card machine, or accepts the consumer's credit card over the Internet using online, real time credit card processing software. The main difference is the variable levels of security involved with the different ways to process credit cards. The following is a step-by-step explanation of how credit card processing works.

INTERNET CREDIT CARD AUTHORIZATION

- Consumer goes to web site, chooses goods and/or services, and fills out the merchant commerce application

- Consumer enters credit card information into a secured form that is sent over the Internet via Real Time Online Processing software (i.e. Authorize.net), which then sends the encrypted transaction to the acquiring processor for credit card authorization

- Acquiring processor sends transaction to card association, which in turn sends the request for credit card authorization to the issuing bank

- Issuing bank accepts or declines the credit card transaction and sends message to the card association

- The card association contacts the credit card processor with the credit card authorization, and then the request to deliver goods and services is given to the merchant by way of the online credit card processing software

- Merchant sends the credit card processing company "fulfillment notification to permit settlement" meaning that the goods and services have been delivered or are ready to be shipped

- The capture takes place when the credit card authorization information is given to the issuing bank and the consumer's credit card is charged for goods and services requested/received

  ** This entire process takes place in less than ten seconds.

Finally, when the merchant decides to settle batch, the acquiring processor finalizes the credit card transaction with the issuing bank and they transfer money into the merchant's bank

WHAT IS A CHARGE BACK?

When a customer complaint about a particular credit card transaction is registered, the issuing bank will usually send a Retrieval Request to your credit card processing company. Your credit card processor will then send it on to your merchant services account. There are some cases in which a chargeback is automatically sent before the retrieval request, but again, that is rare. The retrieval request gives the merchant the opportunity, without being charged, to prove that goods and services were delivered. The best way that a merchant can prove that the customer has made a mistake is by presenting a signed credit card sales draft. If the merchant can produced the authorized signature then the complaint is usually dropped.

If the merchant is not able to prove that the credit card transaction is legitimate, then a chargeback is issued. The card association/issuing bank takes the credit card transaction amount out of the merchant's bank and credits the customer's credit card account. All chargebacks are put on record at the merchant's bank. They can severely damage a merchant services account if too many occur.

Card Payment Systems notifies the merchant account as soon as a chargeback is issued, before the credit card transaction is removed from the merchant's bank. If the merchant services account is issued a chargeback but is able to prove that the transaction is legitimate, the money will be placed back into the merchant's account. If the customer issues yet another chargeback for the same credit card transaction, then a Type III chargeback occurs. This can lead to legal action if an agreement is not made concerning the credit card transaction in question.

A merchant's reserve account cannot be used to pay for a chargeback. This account is put in place as a security issue for the acquiring bank and/or credit card processing company.

The only protection that the credit card processing company offers the merchant services account against chargebacks is a notification of suspicious charges to a particular credit card. If the same amount has been charged to one credit card several times in a row, the credit card processor will not go ahead with the credit card authorization. The merchant services account will always be notified of such a situation.

Because of the way in which the credit card processing system is set up, the merchant services account must be committed to doing all that is necessary to prevent questions of trust arising when a credit card transaction has taken place. In other words, it is the merchant's responsibility to protect themselves against chargebacks and/or fraudulent credit card users.

THIRD PARTY ACCOUNTS

Accepting credit cards is an essential feature for any online business. And every serious business has their own merchant account.

However, many start-ups and small, mom and pop businesses can simply not justify the minimum cost per month if they aren't making the sales to support it yet. As such, we have included this section on third-party processors to aid you in your decision.

Keep in mind that Third Party Processors sometimes:

- Cost disproportionately more the more sales you make

- Require your customers to leave your site to make a purchase

- List their logo on your payment page

- Include their name on your customers' credit card statements, making it more difficult for your customers to remember what the charge is for, which can result in more charge backs, lost sales, and fees.

If you want to sell online, you need to be able to accept credit card payments. The traditional way is to open a merchant account. However, opening a merchant account is expensive, especially for small businesses who are just starting. In the last few years, however, a number of companies have entered the market with a new concept: third party credit card processing services (for example, Paypal). This option offers small businesses a quick and easy way to accept credit card payments. It bypasses the need to open a merchant account, plus, the sign-up process is much easier and faster: you can literally sign-up, be approved and start accepting payments online in minutes.

Third party credit card services usually just charge a percentage of sales and, in some cases, a per-transaction fee, so you only pay when you sell something.

If your sales volume is not very high, a third party service can save you money.

For example, lets assume that you make 10 sales a month at $25 per sale, to compare the merchant account option vs. the third party option:

If a merchant account charges you a $25 monthly minimum fee, $50 in gateway and connection fees, a discount rate of 2.0% of sales, and a fee of $0.30 per transaction (for simplicity's sake we're not factoring in any application fee or set-up fee), the charges you would have to pay your merchant account provider amount to $83.00.

If you use a third party service that, like Paypal, charges you 2.9% of sales plus $0.30 per transaction, it would only cost you $10.25.

However, the advantages of using a third party service start to diminish as your sales start growing. In other words, since the discount rate charged by traditional merchant account providers is lower than the percentage of sales charged by third parties, the higher your sales the more the fixed fees of the merchant account will be offset by its lower discount rate.

For example, let's assume that instead of making 10 sales per month, you make 1000 sales, at the same $25 dollars per sale (total sales per month: $25,000). You will then have to pay your merchant account provider $850.00 (the $25 minimum will be waived because the dollar amount of the discount rate will be greater than $25).

If you use the third party service, you will pay $1025 for the same $25,000 in sales.

Your break even point in this example would be 222 transactions (sales) of $25 dollars each: if you make 222 sales or less, you would be better off with a third party service. If you make 223 sales or more, your best bet would be a merchant account.

In summary, the more you sell the more you should consider opening your own merchant account. However, if you are a small business just beginning to market your products on the net, or if you want to start quickly and don't expect huge sales in the near future, you may want to go the third party route.

The two best-known third party credit card services among web marketers are Paypal and Clickbank.

PayPal began in 1999 as a tool for transferring money for payment in eBay auctions and is currently the most popular online payment system of its kind, with over 35 million accounts at the time of this writing (December 2003), and a fee structure of 2.2%—2.9% of sales plus $0.30 per transaction.

Clickbank specializes in serving web marketers that sell digital products, which are directly downloaded from the Internet. These products are offered through Clickbank's extensive network of over 100,000 affiliate sites. Merchants of digital products simply place a sales link on their site and Clickbank handles the credit card processing. At the time of this writing, Clickbank charged a one-time $49.95 set-up fee, a processing fee of 7.5% of sales and a $1 fee per transaction.

In summary, check all your options first and choose the one that is most likely to fit your needs in the long run. Remember that cost is only one of the variables you should consider in your analysis. Spending some time visiting the websites of merchant account providers and third party credit card service providers, and doing your due diligence early, can save you thousands of dollars in the future.

http://www.adultcardprocessing.com/

http://www.cardsgate.com/

http://www.ccbill.com/

http://www.adultdialersolution.com/

http://www.jettis.com/

How do search engines work?

Search engines help people find relevant information on the Internet. Major search engines maintain huge databases of web sites that users can search by typing in some text.

To compile their databases, search engines rely on computer programs called "robots" or, more specifically, "spiders." These programs "crawl" across the web by following links from site to site and indexing each site they visit. Each search engine uses its own set of criteria to decide what to include in its database. For example, some search engines index each page in a web site, while others index only the main page.

Also unique are the criteria each individual search engine uses to organize information for its users. Some list the results of a user's search according to which sites have the most links from other sites—a system known as link popularity. Other search engines prioritize results according to the summary information contained in sites' meta tags, and still others look for common themes used throughout a site. There are many other ways to organize results, and most search engines use a combination of several of them.

DIRECTORIES—A WHOLE NEW BALLGAME

Directories are often confused with search engines, but actually they're completely different. Instead of using spiders to crawl the web, directories such as Yahoo! and Open Directory Project have real people who review and index their links. They also require web sites to adhere to rigid guidelines in order to be included in their indexes. As a result, directories' indexes tend to contain a comparatively small number of high-quality links.

The factors that influence search engine rankings simply don't apply to directory rankings. Instead, directory editors look at the quality of a site: its functionality, content and design. That means that webmasters hoping to see their sites listed on directories have to use very different strategies than for search engine placement.

HYBRID SEARCH ENGINES: THE NEW GENERATION

Hybrid search engines combine a directory with a search engine to give their visitors the most relevant and complete results. Today the top ten search sites are hybrids. For example, Yahoo! Started out as a directory, but now it supplements its manually compiled listings with search results from Google, a search engine. On the other hand, Google uses Open Directory Project's directory to enrich its automatically generated listings.

Other search engine/directory partnerships work the same way. Learn more about search engine partnerships here.

As someone trying to achieve higher search engine rankings, your goal should be to learn more about influencing factors and how each engine uses them. After completing your research you will have a better understanding of search engines and directories. You will also have an idea of what it takes to achieve a top-20 ranking on major search engines.

This section offers detailed explanations of placement factors used by search engines and directories, as well as tips for their implementation.

DIFFERENT ENGINES, DIFFERENT RANKINGS

Every search engine uses its own unique formula, called an algorithm, to index and score web sites. Search engines' algorithms weigh various factors, such as a page's design and links, to rank pages in their search results. By constantly refining and improving their algorithms, search engines hope to give their visitors the most relevant results.

Many search engines form partnerships and buy technologies to improve their algorithms. They combine many factors and place different weight on each one.

Webmasters who want their sites to achieve a Top 20 position spend a lot of time studying different algorithms. Even when several search engines rely on similar factors in composing their rankings, they may still rank the same site differently. For example, imagine two search engines both use meta tags and keyword frequency as their only ranking factors. If the first one weights meta tags as 70% of a site's value and keyword frequency as 30%, and the second one does the opposite, their results will be completely different.

Understanding ranking factors

Before you can understand how each search engine scores web sites, you need to understand the various factors they consider. These factors can be divided into two categories: **page-related** and **outside**.

Page-related factors are concerned with keywords and their placement in the HTML. These factors include:

- Format, placement and content of the title tag

- Keyword frequency, weight, prominence and proximity

- Use of the meta description tag

- Use of ALT tags

- Use of comment tags

- Use of keywords in URL names

- Alphabetical placement

USING YOUR HTML TITLE EFFECTIVELY

What is an HTML Title and why should I use it?
An HTML Title describes the contents of your web page in one sentence. It's likely to appear in search engines' results and in bookmarks. It's also the first thing a search engine's spider sees on your page. Since your title will be seen by both readers and search engines, it's particularly important.

Your title is the most important part of your page as far as search engines are concerned. Note that **every search engine supports the title tag to some extent.**

Important: Your title should appear right after the <head> tag. If you're using a WYSIWYG (What-You-See-Is-What-You-Get) tool, such as FrontPage, you may want to make sure your title is placed correctly. Having your title placed below its usual place may decrease its power and cost you rankings.

Avoid spam
Don't repeat the same keyword in your title more than twice; it's considered spam. Also, some engines penalize for using all CAPS.

USING THE META DESCRIPTION TAG

What is the meta description tag and why should I use it?
The meta description tag describes your site's content, giving search engines' spiders an accurate summary filled with multiple keywords.

Note: Meta tags are hidden in a document's source, invisible to the reader. Some search engines, however, are able to incorporate the content of meta tags into their algorithms. No engines penalize sites that use meta tags properly, so it's recommended that you always include them.

The meta description tag is especially important because it's the only tag supported by some engines.

Here's an example of a meta description tag:

```
<html>
<head>
<meta name="description" content="Your site's summary here">
</head>
</html>
```

The meta description tag and search engines
A meta description tag can boost your rankings on some engines. To see engines that use meta description tags, click here.

Another reason the meta description tag is important is that some engines use it as a site's summary on their results pages. If they do, the ***reader may actually see this hidden tag***. Make sure its contents are enticing to the reader.

Keywords in the meta description tag
The meta description tag should contain multiple keywords organized in a logical sentence. Place the keywords at the beginning of your description and close to each other to achieve the best possible rankings.

The length of the meta description tag
Search engines vary in their preferred size for meta tags. Try to use the smaller number, 150 characters, for your site. Never make your meta tag more than 250 characters long because some results pages will cut it off.

Avoid spam
Avoid repeating keywords more than 3-7 times in your meta description. Some search engines consider it to be spam.

USING COMMENT TAGS

What are comment tags and why should I use them?
Comment tags provide a way for webmasters to make notes right on their pages. They're hidden in the HTML code and so are not visible to the site's ordinary users, but some search engines, such as Inktomi, can index them.

That means comment tags are another **great way to add keywords to your site**, thus increasing keyword frequency, an important factor in many ranking algorithms.

Avoid spam

Search engines don't penalize sites using comment tags to boost keyword frequency. However, the general rule is not to repeat the same keyword more than 3-7 times in a tag. So, to be on the safe side, follow that rule in comment tags.

USING ALT TAGS

What are ALT tags and why should I use them?

You have a web site. You or Your designer did an excellent job and it looks great. You have plenty of images, including one containing your business name, logo and slogan.

Though your site may look fine, it's not optimized to score high with search engines. Since search engines don't index images, they won't index any text your web site presents in image format—in this case the above-mentioned business name and slogan. To fix this problem, there are ALT tags, which are basically images' descriptions.

Always add ALT tags to your images to make sure search engines recognize all the content on your site. ALT tags filled with keywords can also be used to boost your keyword frequency and help you achieve better rankings.

Avoiding spam

Search engines don't penalize for using ALT tags or even for packing them with keywords. Still, to be safe you should adhere to the generally accepted rule of not repeating keywords more than 3-7 times.

KEYWORDS IN THE URL NAME

What is a URL name?

The URL name is the part of the URL that comes between "www" and ".com." It's the name of a site. For example, in the case of the URL http://www. yoursitename.com, the URL name is "yoursitename."

Why should I have keywords in my URL name?

Recently, search engines began to prioritize the use of keywords in a site's URL in their ranking formulas. Google and Inktomi are two engines that do this. Google is extremely important because Yahoo! uses it to supplement its search results.

Alphabetical priority and its influence

Some smaller search engines use alphabetical hierarchy in their ranking formulas. Also, directories such as Yahoo! and Open Directory Project list sites in alphabetical order.

Avoid spam

Although directories may penalize you for misrepresenting your company's name, neither search engines nor directories will penalize you for inconsistent URL names. This means you can buy any second level domain name you want (as long as you don't infringe on others' trademarks and so on) and search engines will not penalize you for it.

THE IMPORTANCE OF ALPHABETICAL PRIORITY

What's alphabetical priority and why should I worry about it?

Alphabetical priority is a way of ordering files based on the alphabetical hierarchy of the characters in their names. Simply put, it's why some search engines will list a file named "aaa.html" before a file named "bbb.html."

Some search engines use alphabetical priority in their ranking formulas. Also, **directories** list sites in alphabetical order.

Alphabetical characters and others
The commonly accepted alphabetical hierarchy consists of more than just letters. It includes special characters and numbers that can rank higher than an "A".

This means search engines using alphabetical hierarchy will rank a file named "@ABC" higher than a file named just "ABC."

Capitalizing on alphabetical hierarchy in your site

1. **Finding a URL name**
   If you're still looking for a URL name to buy, keep alphabetical hierarchy in mind. Choose a name beginning with special characters or numbers if possible. Otherwise, choose something as close to the beginning of the alphabet as possible.

   If you have a widely recognized trademark, such as Microsoft, use that as your site name. However, if you're company is called Zap Consulting, you may want to find a URL name that has keywords, rather than your exact name, in it.

   Some businesses go so far as to rename themselves to achieve a better listing in directories such as Yahoo! If your company's name starts with a "Z," you may want to add a special character or number to the beginning of your name.

2. **Naming your files**
   Although file names are less important than your URL name to search engine rankings, they can make a difference. Keep alphabetical hierarchy in mind when naming your files, especially when optimizing for smaller search engines. Many small engines prioritize alphabetical hierarchy.

   Example: If you have a choice between naming a file "puppyfood.html" or "food_for_puppies.html," choose the one closer to the beginning of the alphabet. As with your URL name, you may want to add a special character or number to the beginning of file names.

Avoid spam
Don't tell directories your name is "@123acme" when your name is actually "Acme." You risk being rejected on the spot! Remember, directories are reviewed by human editors who can confirm your actual business name.

10 STEPS TO BETTER SEARCH ENGINE PLACEMENT

This FREE 10-step search engine tutorial will guide you through all the moves necessary to design a site with search engine placement in mind. Learn the secrets of creating a search engine friendly, high-ranking site:

Step 1: Find effective high traffic keywords and keyword phrases.

Step 2: Use correctly formatted title and meta tags on all pages.

Step 3: Optimize your content and design for higher rankings.

Step 4: Make doorway pages for carefully selected keywords.

Step 5: Check for spam—and other common SEO mistakes.

Step 6: Register a high-ranking, keyword-rich domain.

Step 7: Discover search engine friendly Web hosting.

Step 8: Add your URL to the top 10 search engines.

Step 9: Monitor and improve your site's ranking.

Step 10: Analyze and understand web log files.

Search engine placement, ranking your site at the top of the search results, can be a time consuming task. This is why many site owners hire search engine placement specialists. Others uses search engine placement software to ease the task.

SEARCH ENGINES

http://yahoo.com

http://google.com

http://lycos.com

http://search.msn.com

http://search.aol.com

http://altavista.com

http://looksmart.com

http://excite.com

Legal Considerations

DEFINING PORNOGRAPHY AND OBSCENE SEX

Before discussing pornography on the Internet, it is useful to discuss what is meant by the term pornography. Defining pornography is complicated mainly because the way it is used in common language or defined in dictionaries is much different than the legal definition of the term. Generally speaking, pornography should be differentiated from obscenity, which is associated with things that are some how repulsive to the senses and is the term most often used in laws dealing with illegal pornography.

Pornography is easily recognized but is often difficult to define concisely. The word pornography originates from the Greeks who defined it as writing about prostitutes. The *Canadian Dictionary of the English Language* defines pornography as "sexually explicit material that sometimes equates sex with power and violence." (1997). This definition, by specifically including the concepts of power and violence, is perhaps too restrictive. Pornography has also been defined as "sexually explicit material that subordinates women through pictures or words". This definition, by strictly associating pornography with the subordination of women, may also be too narrow. The broadest way to define pornography is as a sexually explicit depiction.

A good definition using this approach is from **The Encyclopedia of Ethics**, and defines pornography as "the sexually explicit depiction of persons, in words or images, created with the primary, proximate aim, and reasonable hope, of eliciting significant sexual arousal on the part of the consumer of such materials." (VanDeBeer 1992, 991)

This definition is necessarily broad and covers most dictionary definitions of the term and how it is understood in general use. It is also clear from this definition that not all pornography is illegal, as is clearly demonstrated by looking at the magazine rack of many American corner stores, or associated with power and violence. It may also be seen to include material defined as erotic or materials defined as erotica, although there is no agreement on whether it does or not. However, some material that falls under this definition is illegal and needs to be distinguished from the more general definition used above.

This is where the term obscene comes into play. In the most general sense, something that is obscene is repulsive (though what is repulsive to different individuals and cultures can vary widely) (VanDeBeer 1992, 992).

The *Oxford Dictionary of the English Language* defines obscene as "1. Offensive to accepted standards of decency or modesty. 2. Inciting lustful feelings; lewd. 3. Offensive or repulsive to the senses; loathsome." (1997). This definition is a good starting point, but the main understanding of the term's meaning has no necessary connection to sex (for example war or a messy bed could be obscene) (VanDeBeer 1992, 993).

KEEPING OUT MINORS

Preventing minors from accessing your adult Web site should be an absolute top priority with *every* adult Webmaster. Not only is this simply the right and smart thing to do, it is required by law. Experience has shown us that most adult webmasters take this moral and legal responsibility quite seriously. While it is impossible to keep out unwelcome, underage surfers 100% of the time, there are a few steps you can take to block their entry at as many turns as possible.

Using an adult verification system, or AVS, is perhaps your best line of defense. Most AVS companies, and certainly the bigger companies like *Age Check* and *Cyber Age,* do an excellent job of blocking minor access to their protected sites.

No matter what type of site you chose to build you should strongly consider working with a site blocking company such as *SurfWatch* (www.surfwatch.com) or *Net Nanny* (www.netnanny.com). Once submitted, a site is listed in a database and becomes inaccessible to any computer running the blocking software.

Responsible adult webmasters also take the time to register their site with an Internet rating service. The *Internet Content Rating Association* (ICRA) is a non-profit organization dedicated to restricting access to adult sites. Webmasters submit their site for review and rating. Once the submitted site has been rated and listed in ICRA's database, parents can then set their browsers to block all sites in that rating group of sites. ICRA's Web site is located at www.icra.org.

OBSCENITY LAWS

In the strictest sense, all materials that are considered "obscene" under US Federal, state, or local laws are not permitted on the Internet. Various courts and law enforcement authorities differ greatly in their opinions about just what constitutes obscene material. In general, obscenity standards are based on the standards of the local community. This, of course, makes a prior determination of acceptability enormously complex. Unless you decide to publish "extreme" materials, such as depictions of rape, physical abuse or murder (yes, such sites do exist!), you should be okay. Under no circumstances should you *ever* even think about publishing any form of content that depicts child pornography, bestiality or extreme types of material like those mentioned above. Should you have any questions about the acceptability of any of your content, you need to discuss your concerns with a qualified attorney.

SECTION 2257 DISCLOSURES AND NOTICES

Under Title 18 of the United States Code, Section 2257, and its related regulations (28 CFR Chapter 1, Part 75), adult webmasters and all content providers must be able to produce documentary evidence of the age of all models they show on their Web sites. Before you purchase any adult-oriented content you need to make sure you get the name and address of the custodian of these records. Most content providers will include this information with your order. You should avoid doing business with any content provider who is at all reluctant to provide you with this information.

Federal law also requires that adult webmasters post a notice of compliance on their sites. These notices should be prominently placed on both your Warning Page and your Home Page. The 2257 notice should be placed directly above your copyright notice and should say something like the following:

**This Web site complies with all Federal statues and regulations. (18 U.S.C §
2257 and 28 CFR Chapter 1, Part 75)**
All models are over 18 years of age. Records are available for inspection during normal business hours.

or

**In accordance with federal labeling and record-keeping laws (18 U.S.C.
2257 and 28 CFR Chapter 1, Part 75), the records required by Federal law
for this Web site are kept on file.**

In addition to your 2257 notice, you might consider dedicating a specific page on your site to listing the various Custodians of Record. You can easily link this page to all pages containing the 2257 notice. While this is certainly a good idea, it is by no means necessary.

PRIVACY POLICIES AND USER AGREEMENTS

In short, a user agreement is a document that you, the Webmaster, create to inform visitors and paying customers about any conditions you wish to apply to their use of the site. In some respects, a user agreement or "terms and conditions of use" may be the most important part of any Web site, especially adult sites. Links to your user agreement should be prominently displayed and should appear on your Home Page, and Join Page if you operate a pay site. If you decide to run a site that features both free-access and restricted content, it is a good idea to draft separate user agreements for each area.

A well-crafted user agreement can often help an adult Webmaster establish and define the following:

• Who may use the site—e.g. only persons over 18

• How the site may be used—e.g. for entertainment purposes only

- How the site may *not* be used—e.g. prohibition against downloading materials

- The terms and conditions related to sales—e.g. refund policies and procedures

- The terms and conditions related to any warranties or guarantees

- The limits of your company's liability—e.g. links to other Web sites

- The jurisdiction for any disputes arising from the use of the site

To get a better idea about how user agreements are typically organized, and to familiarize yourself with the type of language used, we suggest you take a look at several examples already in use on the Web.

If you collect any information of a personal nature about people who visit your site or make purchases on you site, the US Federal Trade Commission requires that you have a privacy policy. A privacy policy is a document that you create that tells your visitors how you collect, store and use the information they supply you. A well-written privacy policy will also inform the visitor about how his or her information can be changed or deleted and to whom (if anyone) the information is disclosed and for what purposes. The European Union also has similar, strict regulations concerning the collection of personal information via Web sites.

Creating a privacy policy that is appropriate for you and your visitors is not that hard. You can, of course, write your own using existing models you find on the Web, or you can have one created for you—for free! (For goodness sake do not pay a lawyer to take care of this one.) *The Direct Marketing Association* maintains an online privacy policy generator that is available to anyone by visiting: www.the-dma.org/library/privacy/creating.shtml. Simply answer a few questions; there you have it—a privacy policy you can immediately post on your site.

UNSOLICITED EMAIL—SPAM

Unsolicited emails are commonly referred to as SPAM. While there is some disagreement in the adult industry about the effectiveness (and even the acceptability) of SPAM, we strongly recommend you avoid the practice. Putting the inherently irritating nature of SPAM aside, there are several good reasons to avoid the practice:

- In the US, several states (California, Washington and Virginia) have already enacted legislation that severely limits and/or regulates the sending of unsolicited email.

- Most affiliate/sponsorship programs strictly prohibit spamming. If you are caught—and they do have their ways—you will almost surely be dropped from their program. Additionally, you might find you have been reported to other programs, thereby eliminating your other revenue streams as well!

- Spamming can also affect your adult business even if you do not participate in sponsorship programs. Many online payment processors, such as *iBill* and *CC Bill,* have well-established and stringent anti-spamming policies. Again, if you are caught, you can most likely count on being dropped.

Start Building the Web Site

STOP!

Before you read this chapter complete the following task:

1. 1 Decide what your Adult Site is going to be about.

2. Install and learn Web Authoring Tool. Front Page or Dreamweaver.

3. Choose Your Web Hosting Company

4. Researche your sources for content

5. Learn the basics of Search Engine

6. Chose the revenue model

TO DO LIST

Here's what you need to do:

1. Select your sponsor companies (the people who will pay you) if you are using the free or AVS revenue model

2. Select your web hosting company

3. Obtain your content

4. Create your first site

5. Generate traffic for the site

You're ready to go!

SELECT YOUR SPONSOR COMPANIES

Regardless of which revenue model you decide to start with this step applies to you.

Most certainly if you are using free sites, you will rely on the partnership programs sponsor companies to make money. Also, even if you are creating AVS sites, you should select some sponsor companies for upsells within the content area of your sites. Even paysite owners should use some sponsor companies for additional revenue generation.

You learned that the adult web master makes money when the surfers click on the advertisements of the sponsor companies located in the pages of your free site. Various pay schemes exist with the sponsor companies.

It's possible to paid on a per-click basis. Whenever a surfer clicks on an advertisement, the sponsor company keeps track of each of those clicks and pays the Webmaster for each. As of this writing, 10 cents to 20 cents per click are common, with some sponsors paying less, and some paying more than that range.

Another method of payment is on a per-signup basis. The sponsor company pays the Webmaster for each sales resulting from the Webmaster's free site. Unlike with the per-click basis of payment, it doesn't matter how many surfers. The bottom line in this scheme is the number of surfers who signup to become members. Payment rates vary, but $25 to $45 is a typical range, with of course, variance also going below and above that range.

A variation of the per-signup basis is a percentage partnership program including recurring billing arrangement. The sponsor company agrees to pay the Webmaster a percentage of all current and future revenues generated from the surfer's signup. Recurring billing is monthly (typically monthly, but this can vary) payments that a member pays to remain a member. Percentages vary but 40%—60% is a typical range. The webmaster receives that percentage of revenues from the sponsor company for any surfer who signed up to become a member and who was sent over from the free site of the web master, for as long as that surfers remains a paying member to the sponsor's paysite.

Here is a fairly comprehensive listing of sponsor companies as collected by Ynot with over a 1,000 possibilities:

http://www.ynot.com/

Besides upsells to sponsor companies' paysites, you can make money by selling videos, DVDs, sextoys, dating services and other products.

Here are some sponsors that have (as of this writing) worthwhile products and services for you to sell:

Mall.com: http://www.mallcom.com—Started as an online video sales service but now has a wide variety of products.

Passion Shop: http://www.passionshop.com/Started as a sextoys and adult novelty sales service on the web but now has a wide variety of products and is similar to mall.com

For each of your sponsor companies, make a purchase yourself. Or, if a sponsor has a policy against webmasters buying from their own site, you can have a friend or acquaintance do this for you.

Then, you can track that sale in the sponsor's sales statistics all the way through to when a check is generated and delivered to you.

You want to make sure all the money is there as it should be. If not, you need to do some investigations and/or drop that sponsor.

SELECT YOUR WEB HOSTING COMPANY.

If it's been awhile since you read that chapter on web hosting. From that chapter, you should have a short list of web hosting companies that you can work with.

At this point, finalize communication with candidate web hosting companies and make a decision on one web hosting company to go with.

All of the points in that Chapter apply with regard to selecting a web hosting company. Now that you're closer to home, you should review that chapter and also take heed of the following tip. Insist on a web hosting company that allows you to have a unique IP for your Domain.

This is important for search engine optimization.

The opposite of having a unique IP for your domain is that your domain shares an IP with many other domains of other web sites that belong to other customers of the web hosting company. Typically, all domains in a given server share one common IP.

If that is the case with a web hosting company that is your leading candidate, you need to find a different web hosting company. Companies that don't allow unique IPs are just plain cheap.

A unique IP is important in most search engines. Many search engines carry the domain and IP information of a web page that is registered. Search engines use the IP information as an item to cross-reference in their placement algorithms.

Your web hosting company will setup an account in one of their servers with information on the following:

• FTP login information: server host name, username and password

• E-mail address setup information

• Daily statistics page

If your web hosting company is on its toes, they should be able to set you up within 24 hours tops.

It will take around 48 hours for your domain name to be accessible on the web from the time you had defined the domain to your web hosting company's name servers.

Here is a fairly comprehensive listing of web hosting companies as collected by Ynot.

www.ynot.com

OBTAIN YOUR CONTENT

Since you are starting new in this business, you won't need to purchase many content CDs. In fact, one CD with several hundred images should be enough in the beginning. When you realize that you need more content, you can always purchase more at that time.

So, a purchase could amount in the range of $150 for content CD. As low as $79 for some package deals.

Also, you should be aware that some of the sponsor companies provide content free of charge for your use provided you are advertising their paysites. In this case, you may be able to get away without having to pay for any content at all, which is a definite plus for a new webmaster.

Most of the content providers have web sites that allow you to make online credit card orders and it's possible to receive your order in a matter of days.

Visit www.ynot.com for the list of content providers.

CREATE YOUR FIRST SITE

You have an account in the web-hosting server, your domain name is setup for the server, the content for your first site has arrived and accounts with your selected sponsor companies have been established.

Now, you're ready to lay down some HTML.

Take a deep breath and read some practical tips for professional looking websites.

Select a color scheme and stick to it.

If your are using a logo or preferred colors on its stationery that's a good start. For those of you starting from scratch, choose two or three complementary colors and stick with them—don't change colors on every page.
The most common color schemes include:

- Red, yellow and white
- Blue and white
- Red, gray and white
- Blue, orange and white
- Yellow, gray and white.

If you're not sure what color scheme to choose, surf the Internet and find a website that you like. You can then model your color scheme on what already exists.

Use templates.

Can't find a website you really like? Another option is to choose a template. There are many templates or pre-set designs. These come as part of your web design software (such as FrontPage) or you can check out some websites that specialize in designing templates.

Visit:

www.web4business.com.au emplates1.htm
www.newtemps.com
www.website-templates-resale-rights.com
www.123webtemplatesandmore.com

PROVIDE AN EASY TO USE NAVIGATION SYSTEM.

Warning page. All porn sites should have a warning page to stay clear of legal authorities—and for personal responsibility in preventing minors from entering. The warning page should always be the first page of the porn site.

This is one of the most important issues to consider when designing a website. You need to ensure your visitors can find what they are looking for easily. Most websites either display their navigation bar on the left or at the top. And since most people are used to this type of navigation, it's best to stick with it.

It also helps to include your navigation bar at the bottom of each page to save your visitors from having to scroll back to the top.

DON'T GO OVERBOARD ON SPECIAL EFFECTS

Whilst it is ok to have one or two special effects to jazz up your website, spinning graphics and logos often distract your visitor from the content, not to mention they can take too long to download. Your visitors may click away even before your spinning logo finishes loading.

BACKGROUNDS

Ensure your visitors can read the text on the background, i.e. no black writing on dark blue background or yellow on white. Also be careful that your links are visible before and after being visited. The default for links in most programs is blue (before being visited) and burgundy (after being visited), so if you have a dark background, ensure your links are light.

EXTERNAL LINKS

It is a good idea to open links to other websites in a new window. That way your visitors can easily return to your site when they are finished browsing the external link

SITE MAP & SEARCH FEATURE

If you website is more than 15 pages, it is useful to have a site map or a "Search" feature to ensure your visitors can easily find what they're looking for.

CONTENT IS KING

While it is important that your website looks clean and professional, it is far more important that you concentrate your efforts on the content and promotion.
If you want a professional website, things to stay away from include:

1.   Flash intros, revolving globes, beveled line separators, animated mail boxes

2.   Loads of pop up or pop under boxes

3.   Autoplay music. Allow your customer to play music only if they choose.

4.   Hit counters of the free variety, which say, "You are 27th visitor"

5.   Date and time stamps, unless your website is updated daily or weekly

6.   Busy backgrounds.

Don't sweat the small stuff and get yourself focused on what to include on the website and the best way to promote it. We will cover these topics in future articles.

GENERATE TRAFFIC FOR YOUR SITE

The whole game of making money rests on traffic generation as we're constantly reminding you.

Traffic-generation will play a part in the design of your first site, as your site needs to be built with search engine optimization in mind. Again, this will be addressed in a later more detailed chapter on search engines, but it is important to understand that here.

SEARCH ENGINE STRATEGIES

The most important strategy is to rank high for your preferred words on the main search engines in "organic" or "natural" searches (as opposed to paid ads). Search engines send robot "spiders" to index the content on your webpage, so let's begin with steps to prepare your webpages for optimal indexing.

1. **Write a Page Title.** Write a descriptive title for each page of 5 to 8 words. Remove as many "filler" words from the title, such as "the," "and," etc. This page title will appear hyperlinked on the search engines when your page is found. Entice searchers to click on the title by making it a bit provocative. Place this at the top of the webpage between the <HEAD></HEAD> tags, in this format: <TITLE>Web Marketing Checklist—31 Ways to Promote Your Website</TITLE>. (It also shows on the blue bar at the top of your web browser.) Plan to use some descriptive keywords along with your business name on your home page. If you specialize in silver bullets and that's what people will be searching for, don't just use your company name "Acme Ammunition, Inc." use "Silver and Platinum Bullets—Acme Ammunition, Inc." The words people are most likely to search on should appear first in the title (called "keyword prominence"). Remember, this title is nearly your entire identity on the search engines. The more people see that interests them in the blue highlighted portion of the search engine, the more likely they are to click on the link.

2. **Write a Description META Tag.** Some search engines include this description below your hyperlinked title. The description should be a sentence or

two describing the content of the webpage, using the main keywords and keyphrases on this page. If you include keywords that aren't used on the webpage, you could hurt yourself. Place the Description META Tag at the top of the webpage, between the <HEAD></HEAD> tags, in this format:

<META NAME="DESCRIPTION" CONTENT="Increase visitor hits, attract traffic through submitting URLs, META tags, news releases, banner ads, and reciprocal links">.

Your maximum number of characters should be about 255; just be aware that only the first 60 or so are visible on Google, though more may be indexed.

When I prepare a webpage, I write the description first in a sentence or two, using each of the important keywords and keyphrases included in the article. Then for the keywords META tag, I strip out the common words, leaving just the meaty words and phrases. Google and many other search engines no longer use the keywords META tag for ranking, but it is currently used by Yahoo, so I'm leaving it in. Who knows when more search engines will consider it important again?

3. **Include Your Keywords in Header Tags H1, H2, H3**. Search engines consider words that appear in the page headline and sub heads to be important to the page, so make sure your desired keywords and phrases appear in one or two header tags. Don't expect the search engine to parse your Cascading Style Sheet (CSS) to figure out which are the headlines—it won't. Instead, use keywords in the H1, H2, and H3 tags to provide clues to the search engine.

4. **Make Sure Your Keywords Are in the First Paragraph of Your Body Text**. Search engines expect that your first paragraph will contain the important keywords for the document—where most people write an introduction to the content of the page. You don't want to just artificially stuff keywords here, however. More is not better. Google might expect a keyword density in the entire body text area of maybe 1.5% to 2% for a word that should rank high, so don't overdo it. Other places you might consider including keywords would be in ALT tags and perhaps COMMENT tags.

5. **Use Keywords in Hyperlinks**. Search engines are looking for clues to the focus of your page. When they see words hyperlinked in your body text, they consider these potentially important so <u>hyperlink your important keywords</u>. To emphasize it even more, the webpage you are linking to could have a page name with the keyword or keyphrase, such as blue-widget.htm—another clue for the search engine.

6. **Make Your Navigation System Search Engine Friendly**. Some webmasters use frames, but frames can cause serious problems with search engines. Even if search engines can find your content pages, they could be missing the key navigation to help visitors get to the rest of your site. JavaScript and Flash navigation menus that appear when you hover are great for humans, but search engines don't read JavaScript and Flash. Supplement them with regular HTML links at the bottom of the page, ensuring that a chain of hyperlinks exists that take a search engine spider from your home page to every page in your site. A site map with links to all your pages can help, too. Be aware that some content management systems and e-commerce catalogs produce dynamic, made-on-the-fly webpages. You can sometimes recognize them by question marks in the URLs followed by long strings of numbers or letters. Overworked search engines sometimes stop at the question mark and refuse to go farther. If you find the search engines aren't indexing your interior pages, you might consider URL rewriting, a site map, Yahoo Search Submit Express (formerly SiteMatch), and targeted content pages.

7. **Develop Several Pages Focused on Particular Keywords**. SEO specialists don't recommend using external doorway or gateway pages any more, since nearly duplicate webpages might get you penalized. Rather, develop several webpages on your site, each of which is focused on a different keyword or keyphrase. For example, instead of listing all your services on a single webpage, try developing a separate webpage for each. These pages will rank higher for their keywords since they contain targeted rather than general content.

8. **Submit Your Webpage URL to Search Engines**. Next, submit your page to the important Web search engines that robotically index the Web. Look for a link on the search engine for "Add Your URL." In the US, the most used search engines are: Google, Yahoo, MSN, AOL Search, and AskJeeves. Some of these feed search content to the other main search engines and portal sites. For Europe and other areas you'll want to submit to regional search

engines. It's a waste of money to pay someone to submit your site to hundreds of search engines. Avoid registering with FFA (Free For All pages) and other link farms. They don't work well, bring you lots of spam e-mails, and could cause you to be penalized by the search engines. We'll talk about submitting to directories under "Linking Strategies" below. If your page is already indexed by a search engine, don't re-submit it unless you've made significant changes; the search engine spider will come back and revisit it soon anyway.

9. **Linking Strategies**
   Links to your site from other sites bring additional traffic. But since Google and other major search engines consider the number of incoming links to your website ("link popularity" and "PageRank") as an important factor in ranking, more links will help you rank higher in the search engines, too. All links, however, are not created equal. Links from popular information hubs will help your site rank higher than those from low traffic sites. You'll find links to articles on link strategies in our Info Center (www.wilsonweb.com/cat/cat.cfm?page=1&subcat=mp_Linking).

10. **Submit Your Site to Key Directories**, since a link from a directory will help your ranking—and get you traffic. Be sure to list your site in the free Open Directory Project (www.dmoz.com), overseen by human editors. This hierarchical directory provides content feeds to all the major search engines. Plus it provides a link to your site from an information hub that Google deems important.

    Yahoo! Directory is another important directory to be listed in, though their search results recently haven't been featuring their own directory as prominently. Real humans will read (and too often, pare down) your 200-character sentence, so be very careful and follow their instructions (http://docs.yahoo.com/info/suggest/). Hint: Use somewhat less than the maximum number of characters allowable, so you don't have wordy text that will tempt the Yahoo! Editor to begin chopping. Business sites require a $299 annual recurring fee for Yahoo! Express to have your site considered for inclusion within seven business days (http://docs.yahoo.com/info/suggest/busexpress.html). Other directories to consider might be About.com and Business.com.

11. **Submit Your Site to Industry Sites and Specialized Directories.** You may find some directories focused on particular industries, such as education or finance. Be sure to register with these. You probably belong to various trade associations that feature member sites. Ask for a link. Even if you have to pay something for a link, it may bring you the kind of targeted traffic from an info hub that you need. Beware of directories that solicit you for "upgraded listings." Unless a directory is widely used in your field, your premium ad won't help—but the link itself will help boost your PageRank and hence your search engine ranking. Marginal directories come and go very quickly, making it hard to keep up. Don't try to be exhaustive here.

SELECTION AND PLACEMENT OF BANNERS AND OTHER ADS

Type of sponsor site to advertise. Here's a tip for you *Most of your advertisements should be of sponsor paysites that are in the SAME niche as your free site.*

This should be obvious but is stated here for emphasis. If your free site is about Asian teens, you won't do very well if your advertisements are for a blonde paysite.

Most, though not necessarily all, of your advertisements should be in same-niche sponsor paysites. And the prime banner positions (the first banner of the page) needs to be with same-niche sponsor paysites.

It is acceptable to have other unrelated sites of the sponsor in your link list or in secondary, unimportant positions. You might be able to get some signups of people who are just passing by for porn in general and might have an interest in another category outside of the site's niche.

A money bar is a table of text links to other niches. Each of the links goes to other paysites of your sponsor. Again, it should be emphasized that the primary advertisement position in a page should go to a same-niche sponsor paysite. A money bar is merely an alternative click option in a secondary advertisement position in a page.

Amount of banners and advertisements. You are not in the business of providing free content to the surfers. You are in the business to make money and you are providing free content so that you can make money. *Be very liberal with the amount of banners and other advertisements in your web pages.*

Each and everyone of your pages need to have some type of advertisement, and the more, the better.

The above tip seems intuitive but it has to be articulated because some web masters are a bit hesitant and become conservative for a number of reasons. On one hand, there is the view of being kind to the surfer and offering a worthwhile surfer experience. Also, there is the gun-shyness of some web masters as a result of the policies of some directories in not listing sites with excessive advertisements. The Open Directory Project (ODP) directory is notable in being conservative with excessive advertisements.

On the second point about strict policies of some directories, the point is well taken. So your job is to put up as much advertisement that you are allowed by ODP and other directories and link lists where you intend to be listed. It is a balancing act.

In fact, with those strict directories, try to get away with as much as you can in terms of allowable advertisement without going over the line of rejection.

On the first point about providing a great experience for webmasters, you need to change your thinking on this. Most conventional, small free sites are rarely revisited by surfers, so you need to grab the surfers while you can when they visit the first time.

Also, once the surfer has clicked to enter your site, it almost doesn't matter how great your site is. Your first goal with regard to this surfer has been accomplished; you brought him inside your site (from your traffic generation, marketing work). The next goal is to get that surfer to click on your advertisements.

Get Right, Taxwise

One of the biggest hurdles you'll face in running your own business is to stay on top of your numerous obligations to federal, state, and local tax agencies. A tax headache is only one mistake away, be it a missed payment or filing deadline, an improperly claimed deduction, or incomplete records. And, you can safely assume that a tax auditor presenting an assessment of additional taxes, penalties, and interest will not look kindly on an "I didn't know I was required to do that" claim. The old legal saying that "ignorance of the law is no excuse" is perhaps most often applied in tax settings.

Although retaining a good accountant or other tax professional may prove to be invaluable in avoiding tax troubles, possessing a working knowledge of how the tax systems work is also beneficial. After all, even if you delegate your tax obligations to someone else, you'll still bear the ultimate responsibility for seeing that those obligations are met.

PAYROLL TAX OBLIGATIONS

Take a moment to think back to the day you received your first real paycheck. If you're like many of us, you may recall experiencing some shock upon noticing that the check amount was much less than your actual salary.

A quick glance at the accompanying pay stub alerted you to the fact that your employer had reduced your pay by a number of deductions, the most significant of which were probably the amounts for federal and state taxes. As you're now aware, your employer was withholding from your check the various taxes that you, as a wage earner, had to pay.

Once you become an employer, you too will have to withhold taxes from your employees' pay and to deposit the withheld amounts with the appropriate tax agencies. Furthermore, as an employer, you yourself will also have to pay certain taxes based on the amounts you pay your workers.

Together, those taxes that you're required to withhold and those that you're directly required to pay comprise your payroll taxes. They may include federal, state, and perhaps local income taxes, Social Security and Medicare taxes, federal and state unemployment taxes, and, in some states, disability insurance taxes. And, regardless of whether you employ others, you can also expect to owe some payroll-type taxes on income that *you* receive from your business.

FEDERAL INCOME TAX OBLIGATION

The thought of spending time reading about income taxes probably rates right up there with having a root canal without painkillers. What's more, if you're like most small business owners, you pay an accountant or other professional adviser to handle your taxes.

So why should you spend you're time reading about income taxes? One good reason is that you'll have a much better understanding of the various tax choices that your tax pro may lay out for you. Also, with a little knowledge on selected topics, you'll be able to identify potential tax advantages—and tax traps—in time to do something about them. Wouldn't it be nice *not* to hear your tax pro say, "I could have saved you a lot of money if you had told me sooner that you were thinking about...."

YOUR STATE TAX OBLIGATIONS

When you're running your own business, your tax obligations are never far from your mind. Whether you take care of your own tax matters or have a tax professional that handles your obligations, you and your business are the ones on the line. Tax troubles of any sort are best avoided from the get-go. While keeping abreast of your federal obligations may seem daunting enough, we don't want you to forget about your state tax obligations. All sorts of requirements are imposed on businesses on a state level and complying with them is crucial to your business.

Just as on a federal level, retaining a good accountant or other tax professional can prove invaluable in sorting out your tax matters. However, possessing a working knowledge of your state tax obligations can help you get the most out of your relationship with your tax professional.

Words of Wisdom

According to JD Obenberger of XXXLaw.net—there are eight things you should do if you "want to wear an orange jumpsuit," that is—go to prison. His humorous look at the "silly" and sometimes downright stupid things that webmasters and companies have done over the years is a great way to remember what NOT to do. Learning by the mistakes of others—a great, memorable teacher.

Completely ignore US 2257—Don't keep records, don't keep copies of those records secured at your place of business and a copy with your attorney—don't even bother checking for identification or proof of age.

Create an obscene website—Make something SO nasty that even hardened desensitized adult webmasters will get physically sick from viewing.

Develop a site that appeals to a pedophile—that's right, buck convention and forget your own morals. This is big news in the media, right? Let's go for that popular niche!

Try really to hide who you are—offer disclaimers warning law enforcement officials to stay off your website, work "offshore," etc.

Send skanky spam to everyone—especially blue-haired grandmothers.

Be deceptive—tell surfers that their credit card is used just to verify their age and won't be charged—and then charge it!

Ignore customer service requests—just allow them to pile up and don't bother trying to make the surfers happy.

Steal content—everything is copyright-free and OK to use once it's on the Internet, right?

MORE WORDS OF WISDOM:

Never pay more than $5 per gig to your web hosting company. If you are paying more, there are many better alternative options in the web-hosting world. Failing to understand bandwidth overage pricing has spelled doom for many a web business.

For the work-at-home entrepreneur doing pay site, select only a well defined, easily targeted niche category for your websites. Avoid mainstream categories. You cannot compete with the big boys in the mainstream site arena, especially with pay sites.

Avoid business opportunity programs that entice you to start a mainstream site with a turnkey solution.

Avoid the bestiality fetish for your selected niche. It is illegal in the US.

The Gothic fetish is not recommended for newbie. It is too specialized

Avoid the celebrity niche. The legal hassles inherent in these types of sites are not worth the trouble.

Unless you are an accomplished photographer with ready access to inexpensive models, the most cost-effective source of content is from established, reputable providers of CD's with licensable content.

Don't Use Illegal Content There is no such thing as "public domain" content available for everybody to use commercially in the porn world.

APPENDIX A
Links and References

MICROSOFT FRONTPAGE

http://microsoft.com/frontpage

http://www.accessfp.net/

http://www.anyfrontpage.com

http://www.at-frontpage.com

http://www.intranetjournal.com/articles/200003/fp_index.html

http://www.frontpageworld.com

MACROMEDIA DREAMWEAVER

http://www.macromedia.com/software/dreamweaver

http://webdesign.about.com/cs/dreamweavertips

http://www.andrewwooldridge.com/dreamweaver

http://www.dwfaq.com

http://www.dreamweaverfever.com

http://www.dreamweaversites.com

HTML

http://www.htmlgoodies.com/primers/basics.html

http://kirkhamgate.net/webbeginner/first.html

http://www.alan.clara.net

http://www.powweb.com

http://www.w3schools.com/default.asp

http://www.hwg.org

http://www.weijers.net/guide

http://www.vrwebdesign.org/HTML

http://www.websiteprimer.com

http://www.w3.org/MarkUp

http://www.w3schools.com/html/html_reference.asp

http://www.htmlhelp.com/reference/html40

http://www.ineedhtmlhelp.com

http://cedesign.net

http://www.htmlclinic.com

http://www.htmlgoodies.com

http://www.webcom.com/html

GRAPHIC SOFTWARE

http://www.cerious.com

http://www.photodex.com

http://www.esmarttools.com/ThumbnailBuilder/index.htm

http://www.sipsoftware.com/gmp/

http://www.raizlabs.com/software/magic/

http://www.onfocus.com/snap/index.asp

http://www.linkup.dk/gallery/

http://www.stgsys.com/stgthumb.asp

WEB HOST ACCOUNT

http://www.cozyfrog.com/

http://www.xbiz.com/articlearchive.php

http://adultcheck.com

http://charlie.ynotmasters.com/

http://netmechanic.com

http://hostreview.com

NICHE CATEGORY

http://www.cozyfrog.com/guides/content/articles/NichesExploit.asp

http://xbiz.com/articles/webmastering/1101/14.html

http://www.weboverdrive.com/newsletters/issue104.html

http://www.ynotmasters.com/news/ynews/arch/121400/page3.html

http://www.ynotmasters.com/articles/Niches/

FINDING CONTENT

http://www.web-legal.com

http://www.adultlegal.com

http://allsexinone.com

http://www.exclusivecontent.com

http://www.freshphotos.com

http://www.bestadultcontent.com

http://www.cdbabes.com

http://www.scarlett.net

http://www.sweeterotica.com

http://www.fetishbrokers.com

http://www.xamo.com

http://www.xxxcontentdirect.com

SEARCH ENGINES

http://yahoo.com

http://google.com

http://lycos.com

http://search.msn.com

http://search.aol.com

http://altavista.com

http://looksmart.com

http://excite.com

REVENUE GENERATOR

http://adultcheck.com

http://cyberage.com

http://netverifier.com

http://sexkey.com

http://sexyavs.com

http://freenetpass.com

http://proadult.com

http://universalpass.com

http://adultverifier.com

http://freakpass.com

http://nakedpass.com

http://oneverify.com

http://ageoath.com

http://realavs.com

http://adultsights.com

http://agekey.com

http://ugas.com

http://globalmalepass.com

http://gaypassport.com

http://mancheck.com

http://gaymegasites.com

DOMAIN

http://www.icann.org/registrars/accredited-list.html

http://www.nsiregistry.org/whois

http://www.bulkregister.com

CONSTRUCTING WEB SITE

http://www.maximumcash.com

http://www.trafficcashgold.com

http://stats.adultrevenueservice.com

http://www.siccash.com

http://www.silvercash.com

http://www.ynotmasters.com/listings/adprograms/partner.html

http://www.ynotmasters.com/listings/adprograms/click.html

http://www.ynotmasters.com/listings/adprograms/other.html

http://www.mallcom.com

http://www.passionshop.com

CONSTRUCTING THE PAYSITE

http://www.acpay.com

http://www.glo-bill.com

http://www.verotel.com

http://about.ccbill.com

http://www.epochsystems.com

http://ibill.com

http://www.muiticards.com

http://www.globosale.net

http://www.2000charge.com

PASSWORD PROTECTION

http://www.pennvwize.com

http://www.iisgate.com

CONSTRUCTING QUICK HITTERS

http://dmoz.org/adult/computers/internet/searching/link_sites/
thumbnail_gallery_posts

http://dmoz.org/adult/computers/internet/searching/link_sites/
thumbnail_gallery_posts_2

http://www.ynotmasters.com/listings/hosting/free.html

OTHER USEFUL LINKS

http://www.ynotmasters.com/home.html

http://xbiz.com

http://www.cozyfrog.com

http://www.netpond.com

http://www.adultmasters.org

http://www.adultnetsurprise.com

http://www.adultnet.org

http://www.theadultwebmaster.com

http://www.masterzonex.com

http://sexynet.org

http://www.gofuckyourself.com

http://www.internext-expo.com

http://www.adultdex.com

http://events.xbiz.com

APPENDIX B

Check List

- Have some HTML page generation skills or are prepared to pick it up as you go along and actually have HTML generator software installed in your computer.

- Installed a thumbnails generator software in your computer

- Have a few candidate web hosting companies pre-selected

- Determined your first niche category

- Researched your sources for content

- Attained an understanding of the importance of search engines for traffic

- Finalized your commitment to using a revenue model

- Assessed your competition

- Selected a domain name to start with

- Select your sponsor companies (the people who will pay you) if you are using the free or AVS revenue model

- Select your web hosting company

- Obtain your content

- Create your first site

- Generate traffic for the site

978-0-595-37421-2
0-595-37421-2

Printed in the United States
76581LV00004B/221

9 780595 374212